MAGIC KINGDOM

MAIN STREET USA
- ❏ Cinderella's Castle
- ❏ Main Street Vehicles
- ❏ "SpectroMagic" Parade
- ❏ Wishes™ Nighttime Spectacular
- ❏ Walt Disney World® Railroad
- ❏ Share a Dream Come True Parade
- ❏ Cinderella's Surprise Celebration
- ❏ Cinderellabration

FANTASYLAND
- ❏ Storytime with Belle
- ❏ Ariel's Grotto
- ❏ Mad Tea Party
- ❏ The Many Adventures of Winnie the Pooh *FP* ❋
- ❏ "it's a small world" ❋
- ❏ Dumbo the Flying Elephant
- ❏ Cinderella's Golden Carousel
- ❏ Mickey's PhilharMagic *FP* ❋
- ❏ Peter Pan's Flight *FP* ❋
- ❏ Snow White's Scary Adventures ❋

MAGIC KINGDOM

ADVENTU...
- ❏ Pirates of ...
- ❏ The Magic Carpets of Aladdin
- ❏ The Enchanted Tiki Room
- ❏ Jungle Cruise *FP*
- ❏ Swiss Family Treehouse

LIBERTY SQUARE
- ❏ Liberty Square Riverboat
- ❏ The Hall of Presidents ❋
- ❏ The Haunted Mansion *FP* ❋

EPCOT

FUTUREWORLD
- ❏ Spaceship Earth ❋
- ❏ Innoventions (East and West) ❋
- ❏ Ellen's Energy Adventure ❋
- ❏ Wonders of Life Pavilion ❋
- ❏ Body Wars ❋ 👥-40"
- ❏ Cranium Command ❋
- ❏ The Making of Me ❋
- ❏ Mission: SPACE *FP* ❋ 👥-44"
- ❏ Test Track *FP* ❋ 👥-40"
- ❏ The Living Seas Pavilion ❋

- ❏ Turtle Talk with Crush ❋
- ❏ Soarin' *FP* ❋ 👥-40"
- ❏ Living with the Land *FP* ❋
- ❏ Circle of Life ❋
- ❏ "Honey I Shrunk the Audience" *FP* ❋
- ❏ Journey into Imagination ❋
- ❏ ImageWorks - The Kodak "What If" Labs ❋

GENERAL INFORMATION

MEAL PLANS

Restaurant: _____ Date: _____
Confirmation #: _____ Time: _____

Restaurant: _____ Date: _____
Confirmation #: _____ Time: _____

Restaurant: _____ Date: _____
Confirmation #: _____ Time: _____

DISNEY-MGM STUDIOS

HOLLYWOOD BOULEVARD
- ❏ The Great Movie Ride ❋
- ❏ Disney Stars and Motor Cars Parade

VINE STREET
- ❏ Indiana Jones™ Epic Stunt Spectacular *FP*
- ❏ Star Tours *FP* ❋ 👥-40"
- ❏ Sounds Dangerous— Starring Drew Carey ❋
- ❏ ATAS Hall of Fame Plaza

STREETS OF AMERICA
- ❏ Jim Henson's Muppet Vision 3-D ❋
- ❏ "Honey I Shrunk the Kids" Movie Set Adventure
- ❏ Lights, Motors, Action! Extreme Stunt Show *FP*
- ❏ Al's Toy Barn

LOST CHILD

MY NAME IS: _____

MY PARENTS: _____

MY HOTEL: _____

MY PHONE: _____

ANIMAL KINGDOM

THE OASIS
- ❏ The Oasis Trails

DISCOVERY ISLAND®
- ❏ The Tree of Life
- ❏ It's Tough to Be a Bug!® *FP* ❋
- ❏ Discovery Island™ Trails
- ❏ Mickey's Jammin' Jungle Parade ❋

CAMP MINNIE-MICKEY
- ❏ Festival of the Lion King ❋
- ❏ Camp Minnie-Mickey Greeting Trails
- ❏ Pocahontas and Her Forest Friends

AFRICA
- ❏ Kilimanjaro Safaris® *FP*
- ❏ Pangani Forest Exploration Trail®

LOST CHILD

MY NAME IS: _____

MY PARENTS: _____

MY HOTEL: _____

MY PHONE: _____

MAGIC KINGDOM

FRONTIERLAND
- [ ] Big Thunder Mountain Railroad *FP* 👫-40"
- [ ] Splash Mountain® *FP* 👫 - 40"
- [ ] Country Bear Jamboree ✳
- [ ] Frontierland® Shootin' Arcade
- [ ] Tom Sawyer Island

MAGIC KINGDOM

TOONTOWN
- [ ] Toontown Hall of Fame ✳
- [ ] Judge's Tent ✳
- [ ] Donald's Boat
- [ ] The Barnstormer at Goofy's Wiseacre Farm 👫-35"
- [ ] Mickey's Country House
- [ ] Minnie's Country House

TOMORROWLAND
- [ ] Tomorrowland® Indy Speedway 👫-52"
- [ ] Stitch's Great Escape!™ *FP* ✳ 👫-38"
- [ ] Space Mountain® *FP* ✳ 👫-44"
- [ ] Buzz Lightyear's Space Ranger Spin *FP* ✳
- [ ] Tomorrowland® Transit Authority
- [ ] Astro Orbiter
- [ ] The Timekeeper ✳
- [ ] Walt Disney's Carousel of Progress ✳
- [ ] Galaxy Palace Theater

GENERAL INFORMATION

Priority Seating: 1-407-WDW-DINE (1-407-939-3463)
Special Activities: 1-407-WDW-TOUR (1-407-939-8687)

Hotel Name:_____

Hotel Phone: _____

EXTRA MAGIC HOURS

Day	Morning	Evening
Day 1:____	☐MK ☐EP ☐MGM ☐AK	☐MK ☐EP ☐MGM ☐AK
Day 2:____	☐MK ☐EP ☐MGM ☐AK	☐MK ☐EP ☐MGM ☐AK
Day 3:____	☐MK ☐EP ☐MGM ☐AK	☐MK ☐EP ☐MGM ☐AK
Day 4:____	☐MK ☐EP ☐MGM ☐AK	☐MK ☐EP ☐MGM ☐AK
Day 5:____	☐MK ☐EP ☐MGM ☐AK	☐MK ☐EP ☐MGM ☐AK

EPCOT

WORLD SHOWCASE
- [ ] IllumiNations: Reflections of Earth
- [ ] Mexico Pavilion
- [ ] El Rio del Tiempo ✳
- [ ] Norway Pavilion
- [ ] Maelstrom *FP* ✳
- [ ] China Pavilion
- [ ] Reflections of China ✳
- [ ] Germany Pavilion
- [ ] Italy Pavilion
- [ ] USA Pavilion
- [ ] The American Adventure ✳
- [ ] Japan Pavilion
- [ ] Morocco Pavilion
- [ ] France Pavilion
- [ ] Impressions de France ✳
- [ ] United Kingdom Pavilion
- [ ] Canada Pavilion
- [ ] Oh Canada! ✳

DISNEY-MGM STUDIOS

MICKEY AVENUE
- [ ] Playhouse Disney - Live on Stage! ✳
- [ ] Voyage of The Little Mermaid *FP* ✳
- [ ] Who Wants To Be A Millionaire - Play It! ✳
- [ ] Disney-MGM Studios Backlot Tour
- [ ] The American Film Institute Showcase ✳
- [ ] The Magic of Disney Animation ✳
- [ ] Walt Disney: One Man's Dream ✳
- [ ] Mickey Avenue Character Greetings

SUNSET BOULEVARD
- [ ] Rock 'n' Roller Coaster® Starring Aerosmith *FP* ✳ 👫-48"
- [ ] The Twilight Zone Tower of Terror™ *FP* ✳ 👫-40"
- [ ] "Beauty and the Beast"- Live on Stage
- [ ] Fantasmic!

ANIMAL KINGDOM

ASIA
- [ ] Maharajah Jungle Trek®
- [ ] Flights of Wonder
- [ ] Kali River Rapids® *FP* 👫 - 38"
- [ ] Expedition Everest *FP* 👫

RAFIKI'S PLANET WATCH
- [ ] Wildlife Express Train
- [ ] Affection Section
- [ ] Conservation Station ✳
- [ ] Habitat Habit

DINOLAND U.S.A.®
- [ ] DINOSAUR *FP* ✳ 👫 - 40"
- [ ] The Boneyard®
- [ ] Tarzan™ Rocks!
- [ ] TriceraTop Spin
- [ ] Primeval Whirl® *FP* 👫 - 48"
- [ ] Fossil Fun Games
- [ ] Cretaceous Trail

Plan Your
Walt Disney
World® Vacation
...In No Time

Doug Ingersoll

que®

800 East 96th Street,
Indianapolis, Indiana 46290

Plan Your Walt Disney World® Vacation In No Time

International Standard Book Number: 0-7897-3402-8

Library of Congress Catalog Card Number: 2005927052

Printed in the United States of America

First Printing: August 2005

08   07   06   05   4   3   2   1

Trademarks

All terms mentioned in this book that are known to be trademarks or service marks have been appropriately capitalized. Que Publishing cannot attest to the accuracy of this information. Use of a term in this book should not be regarded as affecting the validity of any trademark or service mark.

The names of attractions and theme parks mentioned in this book are registered trademarks of the Walt Disney Company unless noted otherwise.

Warning and Disclaimer

Every effort has been made to make this book as complete and as accurate as possible, but no warranty or fitness is implied. The information provided is on an "as is" basis. The author and the publisher shall have neither liability nor responsibility to any person or entity with respect to any loss or damages arising from the information contained in this book. Please note that travel information changes frequently, so you should confirm specific details when making travel arrangements. The author has made every effort to ensure the accuracy of the information contained herein. Ratings and descriptions of the attractions mentioned in this book are based upon the author's experience and opinion and may not reflect the publisher's belief or your personal experience.

Bulk Sales

Que Publishing offers excellent discounts on this book when ordered in quantity for bulk purchases or special sales. For more information, please contact

U.S. Corporate and Government Sales
1-800-382-3419
corpsales@pearsontechgroup.com

For sales outside of the U.S., please contact

International Sales
international@pearsoned.com

Executive Editor
Candace Hall

Development Editor
Lorna Gentry

Managing Editor
Charlotte Clapp

Project Editor
Andy Beaster

Production Editor
Benjamin Berg

Indexer
Aaron Black

Technical Editor
Michael J. Scopa, Sr.

Publishing Coordinator
Cindy Teeters

Book Designer
Anne Jones

Cover Illustrator
Nathan Clement, StickMan Studio

Page Layout
Nonie Ratcliff

Contents at a Glance

Table of Contents

I Plan the Trip

II Previewing the Parks

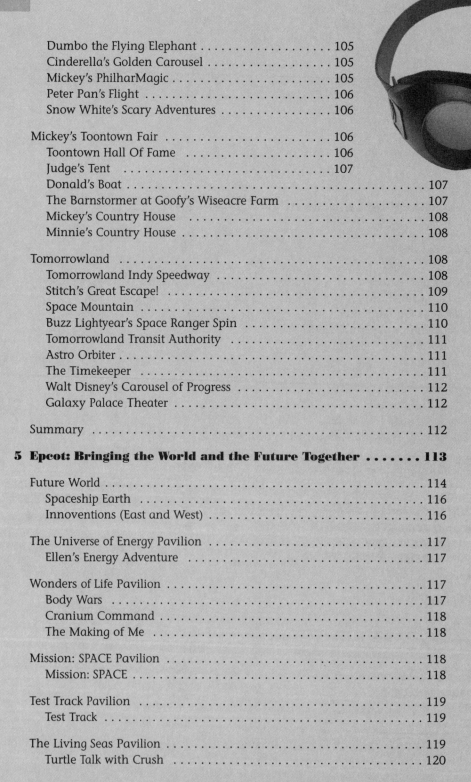

III The Rest of the Kingdom

IV Appendixes

About the Author

Doug Ingersoll is a marketing manager in the publishing industry, involved in the creation and marketing of computer and personal lifestyle books. Doug is from Columbus, Indiana by way of Brussels, Belgium, and has a B.A. in communications from DePauw University and an M.B.A. in marketing from Indiana University.

A lifelong Disney fan, Doug has been vacationing at Walt Disney World for more than 30 years. Over the last decade, Doug has helped friends, family, and others negotiate through the maze of planning and enjoying a vacation to the Magic Kingdom with his unique card system. Doug has refined his attraction, hotel, and restaurant reviews over literally dozens of visits, including family vacations, bachelor weekends, and romantic couple's getaways. Doug and his wife Tracy reside in Indianapolis, Indiana.

Dedication

This book is dedicated to three women:

To my mom, who has always been my best friend, and who showed me how to believe in myself.

To my niece Katherine, who was my long-time dating consultant, and who showed me how to see the world through the eyes of a child.

To my wife Tracy, who is the love of my life, and who showed me how to be a better man.

Acknowledgments

"I thought this was supposed to be a fun vacation for *everyone*."
—D.I., circa 1974

"Uncle Doug, you need a woman. There are lots of women at the beach. We need to take you to a beach."
—K.I., circa 1999

There are so many friends and family that have been supportive in the process of creating this book that it is impossible to thank them all, but here goes.

Thanks to Tracy, who served as initial proofreader and let me go to Disney World so often. Jenni, my sister-in-law, whose first stack of 3" x 5" cards really sparked what is now this book. And to my Mom, Jill, who took us as kids, as well as for many a trip later in life.

Susan Nixon, for reading sample chapters and encouraging me to try this, and Candy Hall for negotiating through the jungle of getting me signed. Margaret Waples and Paul Boger, for letting me write this and still keep my day job. Lorna Gentry, who taught me what I thought I already knew about publishing, and obviously didn't. Michael Scopa, my technical editor, whom I am fairly confident knows more about Disney World than I do, and Nathan Clement, whose art makes me look 40 pounds lighter. Kim Rogers and Andrea Bledsoe, who are the best Marketing/PR tandem you could ask for, and a BIG thanks to the PTG sales reps, whom I have always loved working with.

To my friends at Cisco Press, who taught me publishing, you will always be my family, and to my new team at Que/Sams, thanks for taking me in as one of your own (¡Viva la Booger!).

Finally, thanks to Jamie and Brian Gauker who brought back EVERYTHING they could find in Orlando; to Ed and Donna, the V&A and cruise line experts; and to John for the dried fish—yummy!

And to all my friends and family who came back from Disney vacations and helped with this book through recommendations, comments, maps and support, THANKS! You are all co-authors; we just couldn't fit your names on the cover!

Perge!

We Want to Hear from You!

As the reader of this book, *you* are our most important critic and commentator. We value your opinion and want to know what we're doing right, what we could do better, what areas you'd like to see us publish in, and any other words of wisdom you're willing to pass our way.

As an executive editor for Que Publishing, I welcome your comments. You can email or write me directly to let me know what you did or didn't like about this book—as well as what we can do to make our books better.

Please note that I cannot help you with technical problems related to the topic of this book. We do have a User Services group, however, where I will forward specific technical questions related to the book.

When you write, please be sure to include this book's title and author as well as your name, email address, and phone number. I will carefully review your comments and share them with the author and editors who worked on the book.

Email: feedback@quepublishing.com

Mail: Candace Hall
Executive Editor
Que Publishing
800 East 96th Street
Indianapolis, IN 46240 USA

For more information about this book or another Que Publishing title, visit our website at www.quepublishing.com. Type the ISBN (excluding hyphens) or the title of a book in the Search field to find the page you're looking for.

Introduction

Okay, so you've finally decided to take the plunge and visit Walt Disney World. Whether you gave in to your kids, your parents, your significant other, or your inner child, you are about to embark on a vacation experience that is like no other. With 4 theme parks, 150+ attractions, almost 100 restaurants, 24 hotels, 99 holes of golf, 4 nightclub entertainment venues, 2 water parks, a race track, and every Disney movie character imaginable, there is no doubt that there is something for everyone in your group.

It is this huge list of entertainment options that my sister-in-law Jenni and I were up against when we planned a family vacation a number of years ago. With a group ranging in age from 3 to 60, we had to plan a trip that was "a fun vacation for everyone." But we knew that with so many choices, we could not do it all. That is pretty much where the seed of this book started, on a pile of 3" × 5" cards with notes on rides, restaurants, and everything else we thought might be of interest.

What you will find in this book is the final product of our family's numerous vacations, and the planning that made each trip special in its own way. Some of these vacations had grandkids and grandparents, others were adults-only romantic getaways, and others still involved multiple families. And from those years of experience, we've devised a simple way to plan any group's visit to Walt Disney World.

Using the advice and Trip Card system in *Plan Your Walt Disney World Vacation In No Time*, you can be sure that you hit all of the "must-do" rides that will make the vacation memorable for everyone. This book will also help you by spotting the time wasters that might be great attractions for other groups, but would just be an annoyance to yours.

So let's dive in and plan the greatest vacation you will ever take!

What *Plan Your Walt Disney World Vacation In No Time* Is—and What It Is Not

If you are looking for a detailed history of Walt Disney World, the full menu for a restaurant, or what specific room to request at a hotel to get the best view of the resort parking lot, this is not the book for you. *Plan Your Walt Disney World Vacation In No Time* is not the insider's diary to every last secret that the parks hold. It is, instead, a quick, concise guide to planning and enjoying a vacation to Walt Disney World, knowing that you already have a day job, and it is not vacation planning!

This book takes a different approach than most other Walt Disney World travel books. *Plan your Walt Disney World Vacation In No Time* gives you the basic facts about your entertainment, accommodation, and dining choices. It gives you the essential information to decide if they are right for you, without offering lengthy details or other information that you don't need. The book then provides you a way to record your planning notes with Trip Cards, and in an exercise in ultimate portability, to carry them into the parks without having to take the book along.

Who Should Read This Book

Plan Your Walt Disney World Vacation In No Time is all about real people vacationing at Walt Disney World. The book is designed for people who may have visited the park when they were little kids, as well as for total newcomers who have never been here before. But most importantly, it is for those who know they are sinking a lot of money into their vacation and want to make sure that they get the most out of it, but don't want to dedicate all of their free time to preparing for that trip.

Now, that is not to say that you may not get another Walt Disney World book. There are other good books, and wanting a second opinion is certainly understood. There are also some great websites to use in your overall planning, many of which are recommended in this book. But *Plan Your Walt Disney World Vacation In No Time* can be your overall planning guide, the one that helps it all make sense for you and your group.

How to Use This Book

Now comes the planning. With so many attractions, planning ahead has become a Walt Disney World vacation requirement. So how do you decide what to do? That is what this book is all about helping you do, quickly and easily! In two easy steps, you will be ready to enjoy the wide range of fun that is Walt Disney World, and leave knowing that you made the most of your time.

So what are these two magical steps? The first is planning the broader details of your vacation, such as where you are going to stay, and how you are going to get to Central Florida. This is covered in Part I of the book. The second step is to plan out your time there so that you know everyone in your group will have a great time, and that you won't leave regretting the things you missed. This step is supported by the chapters in Parts II and III.

Basically, you plan the larger issues of your vacation, such as travel arrangements, hotel room reservation, and so on, using Part I as your guide. Then, with the *Trip Cards* (see Figure 1) located in the back of the book, you review the park information in Part II, deciding what to ride, and what not to ride. You check the rides that you want to go on, X-out those you do not, and leave the maybes blank. Then, when you are in the park, you will know the basics of each ride, including if it is one that your group wants to try out. Simple, right?

FIGURE 1
The Trip Cards give you a fast, easy, portable guide to what you want to do and see in each of the Walt Disney World parks.

MAGIC KINGDOM

MAIN STREET USA
- ❑ Cinderella Castle
- ❑ Main Street Vehicles
- ❑ "SpectroMagic" Parade
- ❑ Wishes™ Nighttime Spectacular
- ❑ Walt Disney World® Railroad
- ❑ Share A Dream Come True Parade
- ❑ Cinderella's Surprise Celebration

FANTASYLAND
- ❑ Storytime with Belle
- ❑ Ariel's Grotto
- ❑ Mad Tea Party
- ❑ The Many Adventures of Winnie the Pooh ❋
- ❑ "it's a small world" ❋
- ❑ Dumbo The Flying Elephant
- ❑ Cinderella's Golden Carousel
- ❑ Mickey's PhilharMagic *FP* ❋
- ❑ Peter Pan's Flight *FP* ❋
- ❑ Snow White's Scary Adventures ❋

So, to summarize the book's three parts:

- **Part I, "Plan The Trip,"** guides you through the basics of picking the time of your trip, the hotel where you will stay, and other trip essentials including admissions ticket options, restaurant suggestions, and vacation planning resources.

- **Part II, "Previewing the Parks,"** walks you through the four theme parks of Walt Disney World, including the attractions, entertainment and shopping options, and other relevant information. Detailed ratings help you identify what is a must-do for your group, and what is a time waster.

- **Part III, "The Rest of the Kingdom,"** shows you all the other exciting and fun entertainment that lies outside the four parks. From water parks to race tracks to night-time entertainment venues for all ages. You are sure to find that special something extra that will really put the mark of excellence on your trip.

Special Elements and Icons

Throughout the book, as well as on the Trip Cards, you will find icons that identify some important basic information that will help you quickly plan your activities.

Trip Planning Symbols

I have included some symbols that help you identify vacation activities that are widely popular and should not be missed, and planning activities that will make your planning smoother and easier. You'll see these icons located throughout the book:

Must Do!—This symbol marks something at Walt Disney World that you just can't pass up. Rides that you must experience, parades or fireworks that can't be missed, or a dining experience that is out of this world!

Take a Break!—Part of a great vacation is also getting some quiet, relaxing time together. Activities marked with these icons provide an opportunity to relax, re-energize, and connect.

Hidden Magic—With so many things to do at Disney World, it seems unnecessary to have any special additional activities. But these off-the-beaten-track activities can show you a special side of Walt Disney World, give you an experience you would have never expected at a theme park, or provide you that story to tell friends at home about what a cool vacation you planned!

Do It Ahead—Some things at Walt Disney World are just so popular that you need to make reservations ahead of time. These icons mark text that gives you an idea of actions you need to take, and how far ahead of time you have to take them, to make sure there is nothing but happy faces on the trip!

Also, these icons give you a quick, visual guide to important information about Disney's restaurants and attractions:

❄ **Air Conditioning**—This icon indicates that the majority of a ride is air conditioned. A great way to get out of the Florida sun, and still have fun!

❄❄ **Height Requirement**—This icon indicates that a minimum height, shown in inches, is required to ride this attraction. If you have little ones, you may want to find something else that everyone can enjoy.

FP **FASTPASS**—This icon indicates that the FASTPASS system is used on this attraction. You could save valuable time by getting a fast pass and coming back to this ride later, avoiding long line waits.

$ **Cost**—The cost per guest of a restaurant will help you estimate how much your meal will cost, and if it fits your budget. These ratings figure as follows

$: $0–10 per person

$$: $10–20 per person

$$$: $20–30 per person

$$$$: over $30 per person

Attraction Ratings

So what rides should you go on? That is what the ride ratings are for! All of the rides you read about in *Plan Your Walt Disney World Vacation In No Time* are described, then rated according to age-appropriateness and ride type. Then, each ride is rated by five different age groups. You can see what other guests, from a variety of age perspectives, thought about the rides. Ratings are listed for tots, young children, teens, adults, and seniors, each group having assigned the ride a zero to five rating score.

Ride Styles

Check the attraction descriptions to get a preview of each of the rides, events, parades, and so on offered at Walt Disney World. The ride style descriptions, listed here, will tell you what you can expect:

Experience Area/Playground—These attractions are ones that you look at, walk through, and just experience. Often at Disney World, they have an educational bent, such as the wildlife exhibits at Animal Kingdom, or the World Showcase Pavilions at

Epcot that take you to another corner of the world, but sometimes they include children's playground areas as well.

Theater/Movie—These performances may be movies that use combinations of 3-D, live actors, live characters, animatronic figures, or any of an array of Disney technologies that bring the story to life.

Parade/Fireworks—The parades and fireworks displays in all the parks are extremely popular, so make sure you know the times, and get there early for a good spot.

Character Encounter—Meet the Disney characters, get their autographs, and take some pictures that you will cherish forever. Trust me, it will be the vacation highlight for any child (or child at heart!).

Theme Ride—These attractions are rides that might offer some suspense, but are not the roller coaster rides that some would choose to avoid. They are not all necessarily for guests of all ages, but they carry a central theme and can be fun, scenic, educational, and, in some cases, thrilling.

Thrill Ride—These are the roller coasters and other fast-paced rides that may either be a top priority on your list or something that you have to avoid. Just make sure you know what you are getting into, and you will undoubtedly have fun.

Carnival Ride—These rides are much like the ones on the State Fair Midway back home, but at Disney World they are clean and well maintained, and the carny running them doesn't make your skin crawl.

Age Ratings

To give you a rating for each ride, we had riders of a variety of ages score the rides for their level of fun and interest. Our riders used a 0 to indicate the worst score, and a 5 to give the ride the highest fun/interest score. Remember that some 50-year-olds are far more daring than some 20-somethings, and there are 30-year-olds who grow excited over thrills a 7-year-old wouldn't even blink at. So take no offense at the age generalizations, pick the group that best symbolizes your attraction interest, and pick your rides!

🚲 **Tricycles**—This represents children up to the age of around 6

🚲 **Bikes**—This represents children from 7 to 11

🛹 **Skateboards**—This represents children from 12 to 19

🏍 **Motorcycles**—This represents younger aged adults, from 20s through 40s

🛺 **Golf Carts**—This represents adults in their 50s and older

Your Vacation Needs

So now it is time to plan the vacation! Remember, this is simple. Use the information in Chapter 1, "Planning Your Walt Disney World Trip," to determine your visit's budget and calendar, plan your transportation to and around Orlando, and choose your vacation package. Chapter 2, "Choosing Your Hotel: Leisure Rules!" will help you find a great hotel and make your reservations. Then, it's simply a matter of planning your days. What you want to do is the following:

- Review the attraction descriptions for each park listed in Part II.
- Take the cards from the back of the book and ✔ check off each of the rides you want to go on
- ✕ cross off each of the rides that you want to skip
- Read about other activities throughout Walt Disney World (Part III)
- Reserve any meals that you want to schedule ahead of time (Chapter 3, "Dining at WDW—The Real Magic of Disney World")
- And don't forget to follow the advice we offer throughout the book for reserving any special events that you want to schedule.

And you are done! All you have to do is take your cards into the park with you so that you have a handy reference of what you want to do and what you want to avoid. *Leave the book in the hotel room!*

Part 1

Plan the Trip

Planning Your Walt Disney World Trip

Okay, let's get right to it! The planning is not as big a chore as you may think. You just have to be smart about what your budget is and how you want to spend it. After you set the budget and figure out the bigger costs such as travel, lodging, and tickets, then the planning gets really fun. You can even involve other group members to share both the planning process and the excitement.

So how do you plan out the bigger vacation issues? Easy. It just takes a few simple steps.

- Set your vacation budget
- Decide what time of year is the best for your visit, and how you will get there
- Select what hotel accommodations and tickets meet your needs
- Shop for the best vacation packages to meet your needs

This chapter walks you through each of these steps. Next, you move on to learn about some basic vacation strategies and the attractions themselves. That is the really fun part of the planning. But let's take care of the important stuff now!

In this chapter:

* Plan your budget and decide what special activities that will afford
* Figure out exactly when you want to go to Walt Disney World
* Decide how you are going to get to Orlando and get around Walt Disney World
* Learn what basic vacation strategies will help you enjoy your trip

Things You'll Need

- ☐ Calculator
- ☐ Pen or pencil and paper

Setting a Budget

Ugh, nobody wants to talk about the money. But if you spend just a few minutes planning out what you can afford up front, you can spend the rest of the trip enjoying yourself without worrying about what you are going to owe on your credit card when you get home.

Let's take a look at the costs for a typical family of four. I will assume that the family is flying to Orlando and that they will choose a value hotel to keep the spending down, staying for a six-night/seven-day vacation. That's a *long* vacation, but remember that you will probably go for a shorter stay, so don't let the total at the bottom scare you off. This should set a budget from which moving up *and* down in spending should be pretty easy. While the obvious way to lower the cost is to spend less time there, we go through some other cost savers that you can implement, as well as some good places where spending some extra dough can add a lot to your experience. Where appropriate, I've also outlined some hidden costs and hidden savings that can influence the bottom line.

> **note** I've outlined this budget process to give you an idea of the items you'll need to budget for and some approximate prices for each. However, all of these prices will change over time, so you need to get current rates when planning your own budget.

Travel

In a recent survey of air fare from five U.S. cities (New York City, Charlotte, Indianapolis, Des Moines, and Seattle), the price ranged from $155 to $300 per person round trip. Considering price changes due to time of year and city of origin, at these rates you could assume that air fare will cost approximately $200 per person.

Bottom Line: $ 800

Hidden Cost: Airport parking at your home city

Hidden Savings: A little price shopping can get you a lower air fare bill, and planning your visit for a "slower" time of year can also save you more.

Hotel and Tickets

Remember that our family of four is planning a six-night/seven-day vacation at Walt Disney World and will be staying in a value hotel. We will talk later about special combination packages, but when booking value hotel and tickets, this family can plan on the total to come in at $1,500 or greater for the two combined. As you move to more upscale hotels, or tickets with extra features such as passes to water parks and the ability to move from park to park, the price goes up (Chapter 2, "Choosing a Hotel," gives more detailed information about prices at individual Disney hotels and resorts).

Bottom Line: $1,500

Hidden Costs: Park-hopping or water park features added to the tickets, hotel surcharges

Hidden Savings: Staying at a qualifying Walt Disney World resort saves you the cost of a cab or shuttle to and from the airport when you take the free *Magical Express Service* (see "Getting from the Airport to Disney World," later in this chapter).

note Thinking of driving to Disney World? Not a bad idea, and a great money saver, too. You can estimate the gas and possible overnight stop costs on your own, but also consider some of the benefits:

- Easier access to area stores; saving money on groceries and necessities
- Pack as much as you want for the trip; take home as much as your wallet allows!
- Visit other area attractions without waiting on buses, shuttles, or expensive taxis
- Avoid the crowded Disney bus system, getting there on your schedule

But what about parking costs? Well, if you are a guest of a Disney resort hotel, you can park at all of the parks for free. If you are not, the parking runs around $8 at the parks.

Meals

While there are meal plans that you can select when you buy a ticket package, without such plans, this family should budget an average of $50 a day for adult meals, and $30 a day for each of the kids.

Bottom Line: $1,120

Hidden Costs: Snacks and drinks sneak up on you at every corner

Hidden Savings: Taking some drinks and snacks with you can save you $40 or $50 a day

Miscellaneous Costs

Did you really think you would get by without buying some Mickey-imprinted goodies? No, you will need some general spending money to buy toys, trinkets, clothing, and the occasional poncho if you are caught in a downpour. It is best to assume the worst and plan for $20 per person, per day.

Bottom Line: $560

Hidden Costs: There are stands selling things at every corner, making it hard to say "no" every moment of your vacation

Hidden Savings: Give kids a "one toy, one shirt" budget for the whole trip. Let them make the final selection. They get the fun of shopping; you save a lot of money

Total

For this family, the bottom line for a six-night, seven-day vacation is **$3,980.** There are plenty of ways to lower this cost, and several to raise it, but this is a good rule of thumb for what a long vacation will run you. So how can you lower it? Here are a few pointers

- Seven days, six nights is a very long vacation. Consider shortening your stay. You will still see a lot, and can save some money.
- Bring food and snacks when you visit parks so you can avoid more expensive snacks.
- Check for more affordable times of the year to travel. An early December trip dropped costs by more than $250.
- Consider meal plans and other package offers that reduce your overall costs.
- Set expectations with children on what will be purchased in the parks.

Okay, so now the ugly part is over. Now let's figure out the whens and hows of the trip.

To do list

- ☐ Consider Orlando weather conditions throughout the year
- ☐ Find out when the parks are most crowded
- ☐ Plan your trip around special events

When Should You Go?

What time of year you go to Walt Disney World can play an important role in how much fun you have there. You need to consider the weather, the crowds, and your own schedules. Fortunately, there are two things working in your favor. First, the weather in Orlando is pretty good most of the year. Second, Disney and the Orlando area have so many attractions that there are plenty of places for people to go, including you if the mob scene gets to be too much.

Weather Throughout the Year

Orlando has a pretty great climate year around. Some special weather to note:

- The summers get *very* hot and a bit muggy. If you visit between May and September, be prepared to retreat to air conditioning if needed.

- In the months of December through February, Orlando can get cool enough, especially in the evenings, that it stops being t-shirt and shorts weather.

note In the listings in this book, attractions that are air conditioned have a ❄ symbol next to them, so you can retreat from the heat if it gets a bit too hot.

Here are the highs and lows for the year, by month. Consider the lows as a guide to what you will need to pack for those evenings where you go out to play or dine.

Month	High	Low
Jan	72	50
Feb	74	51
Mar	79	56
Apr	83	60
May	88	66
Jun	91	71
Jul	92	73
Aug	92	73
Sep	90	72
Oct	85	66
Nov	79	59
Dec	73	53

As for rain, it starts to pick up in May, and averages 5 to 7 inches through September. Even so, the rain comes during the warmer months when Mother Nature is going to help you dry off. Still, if you are coming during that

note Temperature and rainfall data comes from the website of the National Oceanic and Atmospheric Administration's National Weather Service (www.nws.noaa.gov).

Book online at www.disneyworld.com

rainy season, consider bringing some ponchos. Otherwise, you have to buy some at the parks for $6 each ($5 for kids).

Crowd Sizes Throughout the Year

Walt Disney World's hotel rate "seasons" typically are determined by the times of year when the park anticipates the largest crowds. As you will see in Chapter 2, "Choosing a Hotel: Leisure Rules!" the rates for the hotels change throughout the year. But the crowd sizes don't always reflect Disney's "seasonal" calendar. So when is it busy, and when is it slow? The weekly estimate shown in Figure 1.1 should help.

tip It is recommended that you shoot for times when the crowds are moderate in size. If the crowds are too light, the parks can seem abandoned, which really deadens the spirit of the place. If it is at its most crowded, the lines get annoyingly long and you usually end up missing out on some of the more popular rides.

FIGURE 1.1
Remember that as a rule, Walt Disney World is busiest during holidays and slowest when kids are in school.

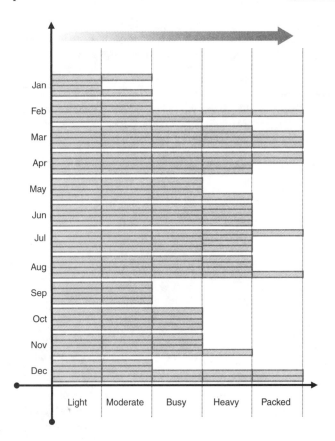

Disney vacation reservations: 1-407-939-7675

Special Events Throughout the Year

Walt Disney World hosts numerous special events throughout the year. This section lists just a few of the bigger ones. Once you know when you are planning on attending, make sure to check the Walt Disney World website to get exact dates and to see what else might be going on when you are there. While these events can attract a crowd, they can offer some great activities, food, and entertainment that are well worth dealing with the crowds.

January: Walt Disney World Marathon

March: Atlanta Braves Spring Training

April/May/June: Epcot International Flower and Garden Festival

May/June: *Star Wars* Weekends

September: Night of Joy

October: Funai Classic Golf Tournament, and Mickey's Not-So-Scary Halloween Party

October/November: International Food and Wine Festival

November thru January: Osborne Family Spectacle of Lights

December: Mickey's Very Merry Christmas Party, Holidays Around the World, Pleasure Island's New Year's Eve, and Atlantic Dance Hall New Year's Eve

> **note** Another gathering at Walt Disney World is the annual *Gay Days*. This event is not affiliated with Disney World, but it certainly packs the Orlando parks and hotels, with more than 130,000 attendees. This week-long get-together is usually held in early June, always capturing the first Saturday of the month. You can pinpoint the dates by going to www.gaydays.com.

To do list

- ☐ Plan ahead to find the right exits when driving to Walt Disney World
- ☐ Learn which airlines fly into the Orlando airport
- ☐ Plan transportation to and from the airport
- ☐ Decide whether you'll need a car while at WDW

Getting to Walt Disney World

There are a lot of ways to get to the popular central Florida area, but the most popular are driving (for those in the Southeast U.S.) and flying (for the rest of us). However you travel, the pointers in the following sections will make your trip easier.

Driving to Orlando

Regardless of where you are driving from, as you near Walt Disney World, the signage is very clear, and you should have no problem finding your resort. Just remember what area your resort is located in (for example, Epcot Resorts Area or Downtown Disney Resorts Area), as the first signs you see indicate how to get to those areas. As you get closer, the signage gets more hotel-specific. Here are the main exits off of US-4 that you will want to keep an eye out for:

Exit 64 and Exit 65

If you are coming from Tampa (Exit 64) or Orlando (Exit 65), use these exits to get to Blizzard Beach, the Magic Kingdom area resorts, the Animal Kingdom Area resorts, and the Wide World of Sports Area resorts.

Exit 67

Take this for Typhoon Lagoon, the BoardWalk, the Downtown Disney Area resorts, and the Epcot Area resorts.

Exit 68

Take this for hotels on Hotel Plaza Boulevard, or if you want to hit the Gooding's grocery store at the Crossroads Plaza shopping center.

> **tip** A great money saver is to bring snacks and beverages to your hotel room from home. If you fly in, but want to stock up on some of these for the room, you can go to the nearby Crossroads Plaza shopping center, where a Gooding's grocery store can conveniently serve as your general store. The center is located at exit 68 off US Highway 4, at the end of Hotel Plaza Boulevard by Downtown Disney.

> **tip** If your travels include special needs and you need to investigate airport facilities, you can find out more at the airport website at www.orlando-mco.com.

Flying to Orlando

The Orlando International Airport (MCO) sees more than 31 million travelers go through its doors in a year, so naturally a large host of airlines fly here. The more notable domestics include AirTran, Alaska, America West, American, ATA, Continental, Delta, Frontier, independence air, jetBlue, Hawaiian, Midwest, Northwest, Song, Southwest, Ted, United, and US Air.

> **tip** The king of transportation in the Orlando area is Mears. Mears runs cabs, buses, shuttles, and town cars. While there are other services, if you need a shuttle, you should consider reserving one ahead of time at www.mearstransportation.com or calling 407-423-5566.

Getting from the Airport to Disney World

To get from the airport to Walt Disney World you can rent a car, take a cab or shuttle, or enjoy the new **Disney's Magical Express Service**. The complimentary express service is an exclusive offering for guests at Disney-owned resort hotels (these services are not available to guests of the Disney Swan and Disney Dolphin resorts).

Cabs run you about $50–60 from the airport to the Disney area, but you can fit in as many as the cab will hold. A shuttle, on the other hand is $29 per person, for a round trip. For our mythical family of four, the cost is pretty much the same, so you should cab it and get there right away. On the other hand, if your group is three or fewer, the shuttle can save you quite a bit of money.

note Disney's Magical Express Service is a new service started in May, 2005. If you stay at a participating Disney resort, you get, at no additional charge, a round trip to and from the airport. Basically, when you arrive at the Orlando International Airport, they grab your specially tagged bags for you, place them on a bus, and then drive you to your resort. At the end of your vacation, they even take you back to the airport! Though many people have been very satisfied with this service, others have found it to be a pretty long and tedious experience. Most of this latter group, however, chalked it up to the "working out the kinks" phase of a new service, and said they would give it another try on their next visit, especially since it is free!

HIRING A RENTAL CAR

Rental cars are available at the Orlando International Airport (MCO) from Alamo, Avis, Budget, Dollar, Enterprise, Hertz, L & M, National, Payless, and Thrifty. The better question is do you need one? If you are going to spend the entire vacation at Walt Disney World, it is likely that your car will sit in the parking lot, costing you money. Instead of renting a car for the entire time, get to your hotel via shuttle, cab, or Disney Magical Express, and just rent a car for a day if you really need one. You can pick up rental cars at the following easily accessible Walt Disney World locations, though you can have one delivered to any Disney-owned hotel as well.

* Alamo on Hotel Plaza Boulevard
* Avis at the Hilton on Hotel Plaza Boulevard
* Budget at the Doubletree Hotel on Hotel Plaza Boulevard
* Dollar at the Holiday Inn on Hotel Plaza Boulevard
* National at the Car Care Center, the Dolphin Hotel, and on Lake Buena Vista Drive

Getting Around Walt Disney World

Disney has an elaborate internal transportation system for guests, combining an enormous bus fleet, watercraft, and the trademark monorails. In Chapter 2, you will see how to get from your hotel to the theme parks, the water parks, and the nightlife areas. Here are the basics of what else you need to know about getting around within Walt Disney World. And of course, if you are staying at a Disney hotel, all of these are free!

Buses

The fleet of buses is the main mode of transportation throughout Walt Disney World. For the most part, they run you between attractions, resorts, water parks, and the nightlife areas. They are usually on a 20-minute interval, so you should not have to wait too long between buses. There are two key hubs for buses, one at Downtown Disney, and the other at the Transportation and Ticket Center near the Magic Kingdom. If there are no direct buses to your destination (such as when going from one resort hotel to another), just grab a bus to one of these hubs and switch over to a bus headed to your destination.

> **note** Transportation Golden Rule: Ask your hotel desk staff the best way to get to a destination. They can tell you what is fastest, and most convenient.

Watercraft

Boats connect several different resorts and attractions. These can be a relaxing and scenic way to get from place to place, and I highly recommend you take them if they are convenient. The major ones to remember are

- *Disney-MGM* to *Swan and Dolphin Hotels* to *BoardWalk* to *Yacht and Beach Club Hotels* to *Epcot*
- *Magic Kingdom* to *Wilderness Lodge* to *Fort Wilderness Resort and Campground*
- *Downtown Disney* to *Saratoga Springs & Port Orleans resorts*
- *Transportation and Ticket Center* to *Magic Kingdom*

Monorail

A Disney trademark, the monorail is still as cool as it was in the '70s. There are two basic loops for the monorail:

- *Transportation and Ticket Center* to *Contemporary Resort* to *Magic Kingdom* to *Grand Floridian Resort* to *Polynesian Resort*
- *Transportation and Ticket Center* to *Epcot* and back

tip *Hidden Magic*

When you are in a monorail station, ask the attendant if you can ride in the front. You will have to wait for the next one that has an empty front cab, so realize you will probably have to let a few monorails go by. But the view really gives you a special moment that you won't forget, especially entering the Contemporary Resort, or gliding around Spaceship Earth at Epcot.

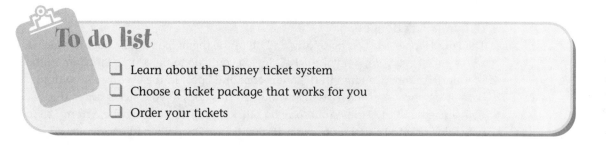

To do list

- ☐ Learn about the Disney ticket system
- ☐ Choose a ticket package that works for you
- ☐ Order your tickets

Choosing and Buying Disney Attraction Tickets

In January 2005, Disney restructured the ticket system to make it easier to personalize tickets to what you need. You begin with a *Magic Your Way* ticket, which gives you basic access to a park for each day you designate (and pay for). After that, you can choose from a number of options to upgrade your ticket. The ticket system can seem complex, but it's not. Let's take a look at how it works and what it will cost you. Also, we can look at other tickets that you might buy, as well as other advance reservations or planning that you may want to do.

Step 1: Pick the Number of Days for Your *Magic Your Way* Ticket

This is your base ticket, good for however many days you purchased it for, which can be anywhere from 1 to 10. This base ticket gives you access to one park per day. If you use your ticket to go into the Magic Kingdom, that is the only park where it will work for that whole day. Of course, the next day you can use your ticket at another park, or to go back to the Magic Kingdom if you wish. Currently, this base

Book online at www.disneyworld.com

ticket ranges from $59.75 ($48.00 for kids aged 3–9) for a single day, to $193 ($155 for kids) for 5 days, to $208.00 ($167 for kids) for 10 days. As you increase the number of days on your ticket, the lower the per-day cost is going to be. For the 10-day ticket, it works out to $20.80 per day. Regardless of how many days you choose for your ticket, from 1 to 10, you have 14 days from the first day you use your ticket to use all of the days on your ticket.

Step 2: Select What Ticket Options You Want

Okay, now comes the interesting part. There are a number of options that you can add to your ticket. As you add them, you add to the cost of your ticket, so make sure you are going to need them. You can add more than one option if you wish, or none at all.

Option 1: Park Hopper

The Park Hopper lets you go to any and all of the theme parks (this does not include water parks) every day on your ticket. So you could go to the Magic Kingdom in the morning, Animal Kingdom in the afternoon, and Epcot in the evening. As with the base ticket price, the longer your stay, the less this adds to your ticket price. The daily increase to the Magic Your Way base ticket price can be anywhere from $35 for a one-day ticket to $3.50 a day for a 10-day ticket. The daily add-on rate for a 5-day Park Hopper option is $7.

Who should use it? Adult-only groups, families with teens, and any group who may want to visit one park during the day and dine at an Epcot restaurant in the evening.

Who should avoid it? Families with smaller children who probably won't make it to more than one park per day.

note You will save money by buying your tickets before you leave home, as opposed to buying them at the parks. It can be a savings of around $20 per ticket on a four- or five-day ticket.

Option 2: Magic Plus Pack

The Magic Plus Pack gives you access to the two water parks at Disney World (*Typhoon Lagoon* and *Blizzard Beach*), the nightclubs of Pleasure Island, the Disney Quest indoor entertainment facility at Downtown Disney, and the Wide World of Sports Complex. The additional cost adds anywhere from $45 for a one-day ticket add-on to $4.50 per day for a 10-day ticket; adding this option to a 5-day ticket costs $9 per day. Note that you do not get *Park Hopper* access with this option, though you can go back to the water parks and other Pack options repeatedly. You are limited in the total number of visits to these added attractions, based on the number of days on your ticket, so check how many special area admissions you get for your money.

Who should use it? Adult-only groups planning to go out on several evenings for some dancing and partying; families with younger kids who plan on visiting the water parks

Who should avoid it? Families with smaller children, or other groups that won't go out for more than dinner at night, or don't plan on visiting the water parks

Option 3: No Expiration Date

This option wipes out the 14-day expiration date recently installed on all Disney tickets, and lets you bring the ticket back and use the leftover days whenever you want. The cost increase is pretty small, but unlike with the other options, the cost gets higher the more days you have on your base ticket. The cost of this option can range from $5 to $10 per day, with the rate going *up* as you add more days.

> **caution** *NO, you cannot give your ticket to someone else. Only you can use it!* New systems at Walt Disney World guarantee that you cannot transfer tickets, so don't plan on passing along extra days to a friend living in the area.

Who should use it? Anyone from Central Florida or who travels to the area frequently and knows they will get a chance to redeem the extra days.

Who should avoid it? Anyone who is even remotely uncertain of when they might get back here.

Water Park, Disney Quest, and Pleasure Island Tickets

If you decide not to get the Magic Plus Pack option, but want to visit one of these attractions, here are the prices:

- Water park tickets are $34 for a single water park 1-day pass, $28 for kids aged 3–9
- Disney Quest tickets are $34 for adults, and $28 for kids aged 3–9
- Access to the clubs of Pleasure Island costs $20.95.

> **note** Premium Annual passes are available for $515 for adults and $438 for kids 3–9 that give access to all the theme parks, water parks, Pleasure Island, and DisneyQuest. Theme park–only Annual Passes go for $395 ($336 for kids).

WEBSITE RESEARCH

Looking to get even more in depth information? Well, the first place you should go is www.disneyworld.com, for the official word on what times parks are open, what rides will be closed for repairs, and just about anything else. But if you are looking for even more information, here are some popular unofficial Disney-focused websites that offer everything from bulletin boards rating the attractions and showing restaurant menus. These are just three of the ones I like to visit:

www.allearsnet.com—Run by Deb Wills, this may be your best next stop. Deb and the All Ears team bring upbeat, honest advice. Her website is a *must-do* visit before your trip—**she should be the CEO of Disney!**

www.wdwmagic.com—This website gets into a lot of photography, and if you become a member of the site, you can practically "ride" most of the attractions via posted videos taken by past visitors of the parks.

www.magicalmountain.net—Lots of forums on different Disney topics, so you can get some great dining or other ideas.

To do list

- ☐ Learn how to book a vacation package directly with Walt Disney World
- ☐ Understand the benefits of booking through an authorized Disney vacation planner
- ☐ Explore possible packages with other Disney affiliates
- ☐ Consider the Disney Dining and Premium package plans

Booking a Disney Vacation Package

Okay, so how do you actually go about booking a Disney vacation? Just as with any other vacation, there are a million ways to book your trip arrangements. You can book it all on your own, via phone or the Disney World website. You can go through a travel agent or a Disney partner organization such as AAA. So what source is the best for getting a good deal? That changes all the time, so make sure that you look at several of the options we describe here, check your Sunday paper for even more special deals, select ones that match your needs, and then pick the one that gets you the best bang for your buck.

Disney vacation reservations: 1-407-939-7675

Booking with Disney

You can book with Disney directly, via their website at www.disneyworld.com, or by calling (407) 939-7675. After undergoing several recent updates, the website seems to be good at finding you the best deals on hotel and tickets, though the air fare options could almost always be matched or beaten by any of the popular travel websites. As for the phone operators, they are actually pleasant (what a nice change!) and also do a great job of finding the deals.

Booking with a Disney-Authorized Vacation Planner

Independent travel agents that are designated as Disney-authorized vacation planners can sometimes bring you some great packages, courtesy of the Walt Disney Travel Company. They are not employed by Disney, but are recognized by Disney as experienced travel agents that can help. The benefits of booking with a Disney-authorized vacation planner are obvious as well; they can help you make all the plans that you need to have for the trip. If you are a seasoned traveler who never uses an agent, you may not benefit from using a Disney-authorized agent. But if you don't travel often, let one of these folks help out. Check their prices, compare them to what you can organize on your own, and you might be surprised by what you can get out of the relationship, including savings!

Booking with AAA, AARP, or Other Disney Affiliates

Make sure, if you are a member of AAA, AARP, or other similar organizations, that you check for their Disney vacation packages. In some cases, their specials can offer some great deals. But make sure you go through the program elements with a fine-toothed comb to make sure that it is the right package for you.

> **tip** If you search using the term "Disney vacations" or "Disney packages" at either www.expedia.com or www.travelocity.com, you can get packages that include Walt Disney World resorts.

Package Specials: Dining Plan and Premium Plan

Most Disney packages offer other package add-ons to sweeten the deal. Always look at the package details and see if they meet your particular needs, as well as if the cost is matched by the package value. Packages come and go, but let's look at two of the most current ones.

Disney Dining Plan

With this plan, you pay a flat amount per person in exchange for a number of meals at Disney restaurants. For this charge, each day you get

- One counter-service meal (1 entrée, 1 dessert, 1 drink)
- One table service meal (1 appetizer, 1 entrée, 1 dessert, 1 drink),
- One snack (ice cream bar, popcorn, or bottle of soda or water)

Most Disney resort and park restaurants are included. A character meal counts just like a table-service meal, but a single dinner show or meal at a signature restaurant (such as the *California Grill* and the *Hollywood Brown Derby*) counts as two table-service meals in this plan. All meal packages are tracked electronically, so you don't need to carry around vouchers or a booklet, though you will want to keep track.

For our imaginary family of four, adding this package costs about $540 dollars, or about $38 per person per day. That comes in just under our earlier dining estimate. So should you go for it? Since our estimate was based on keeping spending down, and since Disney includes almost every restaurant, it looks like a good deal. Just remember that you are only getting two meals a day, not three, so plan accordingly. Bottom Line: This is a GREAT deal!

Premium Plan

The premium package adds a great deal of perks to your ticket, but the cost is pretty significant. First, you must select the Park Hopper and Magic Plus ticket options. After those advantages, the Premium Plan adds

- Breakfast, lunch, and dinner every day, at any restaurant in the dining plan
- Unlimited use of a selected recreation facility (choices include golf, fishing excursions, boating, tennis)
- Passes to Cirque de Soleil's La Nouba show
- Admissions to Disney Children's Activity Centers (see "Disney with Children," later in this chapter)
- Unlimited Theme Park Tours (see Part II, "Previewing the Parks")
- Admission to all Grand Gathering Experiences (specialized large group events)

Purchasing the Premium Plan for our family of four (along with the required Park Hopper and Magic Plus options) added $3,094.02 to the basic cost of our Magic Your Way seven-day tickets. If you take out the added cost that the Park Hopper and the Magic Plus options added, you are still adding around $2,800 to the price. You better be absolutely sure that you are going to use most, if not **all** of these services to justify the extra cost. Of course, if money is no object, it gets you to as close as you can get to an "all-inclusive" vacation as Walt Disney World has. I wouldn't recommend this package, however, for most visitors.

To do list

- ☐ Learn strategies for visiting Walt Disney World with children
- ☐ Learn strategies for a great "adults only" visit
- ☐ Find out how to plan special events at the parks
- ☐ Learn packing and time-saving tips

Vacation Strategies

There are some visitors who plan out every step of their vacation. Are they nuts? Probably a little bit, but there is some method to their madness. Knowing a few simple rules to follow when you hit the parks can help you spend less time in lines and more time meeting Mickey and enjoying the rides. Here are some of the key plans that you should consider following.

note For those times when you do have to wait in line, make sure you are prepared with some in-line fun. Bring something to keep everyone entertained, but without bothering those around you. Make it something that you can do while you are continually moving. Suggestions include cards, traveling versions of board games such as backgammon, and electronic handheld games.

Things You'll Need

- ☐ Trip Cards from this book
- ☐ Pencil/pen

General Strategy #1: Plan Your First Day's Activity

Odds are that the day you arrive in the Orlando area, you will not be getting there first thing in the morning, rested and ready for a day at a theme park. For most, it is an afternoon arrival via plane, with some time needed to settle in to the hotel. Remember of course that if you hit a park, you will "spend" one day of your tickets, so it may be better to save that for another day where you can go for the whole day.

Book online at www.disneyworld.com

So make sure that you plan something different that will start the vacation off with a bang! Some ideas include

- Hit your hotel pool for a relaxing dip, then dinner somewhere fun
- Try kick-starting your Disney experience with a character meal or dinner show, such as the Luau (Spirit of Aloha) or the Hoop De Doo Review
- Take your first Monorail ride!
- Go clubbing at Pleasure Island
- Take in a fireworks show by watching Epcot's from the BoardWalk
- Go to Downtown Disney or the BoardWalk for dinner

General Strategy #2: Plan Your Parks and Meals

Flexibility and spontaneity can make the vacation fun, but you should still work a little advance planning into your days at Disney. You really should plan out what parks you intend to visit (or whatever other activity you have in mind) on each day of your trip, as well as at least some of your meals. Use the Trip Cards and the park and restaurant descriptions in this book to help make these plans.

You should consider what parks are open for Extra Magic Hours on those days, as well as how long you plan on staying at each. Each of the parks seems to be more crowded during certain days of the week. The "busy days" are traditionally as follows:

- Magic Kingdom: Mondays, Thursdays, and Saturdays
- Epcot: Fridays
- Disney-MGM: Sundays and Wednesdays
- Animal Kingdom: Tuesdays

Once you have the general agenda of what park you will visit on which days, then you should plan out some of your meals. You can get your character meals, dinner shows, and romantic soirées planned out, as well as reserved ahead of time.

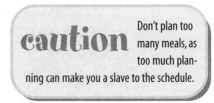

caution Don't plan too many meals, as too much planning can make you a slave to the schedule.

Disney with Children

If you are bringing kids to Walt Disney World, you are in the majority. That does not mean, however, that you always have to be in the longest lines and at the busiest restaurants. Here are some strategies that can help you avoid crowds and maximize the fun.

Before You Leave

I have had friends who surprised their kids by not telling them they were headed to Walt Disney World until they literally were there, and it was great. But you can have fun at the other extreme by following these strategies:

- Let your kids help with the planning, from selecting which hotel in your price range would be most fun, picking what restaurants they want to go to, and filling out the Trip Cards and selecting what attractions to hit and which to miss.

- Craft projects can include making "Lost Child" lanyards that they can wear in the parks, as well as making matching family T-shirts that help keep everyone together. Try tie-dye or some other kind of unique decoration.

Once You Are There

After you get to Walt Disney World, use these strategies to make the trip more enjoyable for you *and* your children:

- Regardless of age, make sure that most days include a pool visit or nap in the afternoon. Despite their apparently endless supply of energy, kids will tire out, and if you don't plan for that, you will have some very unpleasant days at the end of the vacation.

- Know your child's height before you go and determine what rides you can't let them experience, avoiding some disappointment ahead of time.

- Each theme park has a Baby Care Center where you can retreat to an air-conditioned calm zone. There are TVs running Disney movies, toys, baby changing areas, and other conveniences that can allow you to calm an upset child or rest a tired one.

- Read the "Rider Switch" section later in this chapter to see how you can enjoy those rides that your kids can't go on.

- Use the Lost Child cards in the back of the book to help in case you are separated.

- Identify an easy-to-find landmark where everyone can meet if they get separated.

- Have autograph books at the ready *before* you get to the parks, in case you meet some characters at the hotel or elsewhere.

- Plan a character meal. It is a must-do for 99.9% of all children.
- Consider the Children Activity Centers or babysitting services as a way to get some away-from-the-kids time, without ruining the fun for them. Sane mommy and daddy equals a happier vacation for all!
- Personally, I don't think you should take kids to the clubs of Pleasure Island, but if you do, take the older teens to *Motion*, and remember that the later the showing at the *Comedy Warehouse*, the more risqué the humor.
- Ride in the front of the monorail.
- Trust teens with some independence. Give them some time alone in a park with a planned meeting place and time. They will appreciate it, and you will get a report on some activities you may want to try yourself.

> **tip** In many theater-seating attractions, people will elbow others out of the way to get to the front of the crowd, waiting by the doors that lead to the theater. Let them go! In most cases, being in the middle of the crowd means you will sit in the middle of the theater, where 3D effects are best, and the view of all characters is guaranteed. Let the piggies sit on the sides where they deserve to be!

After You Get Home

Capture that magic! Have kids make albums of their trip, complete with photographs, tickets, menus, hotel and park maps, and anything else you can think of. If you need some extra scrapbooking materials, visit *Disney's Wonderful World of Memories* store at Downtown Disney.

Disney with Adults Only

Disney World is not just for kids; in fact, it is now considered the number-one honeymoon destination in the United States. There is fun to be had for adult groups, as well as romance for couples who are so inclined. There are also some strategies that will help you shorten line waiting time, see more, and enjoy the trip as a full vacation. Here are some pointers to remember when preparing for your visit.

Adult Group Strategies

Use these strategies to make the most of your kid-free fun at WDW:

- Kids get tired by the mid-afternoon, leaving a less crowded park for the adults. You should consider arriving at the parks a little later in the morning, making sure that you are hitting your peak in the afternoon. Lines will shorten as the tikes head to their hotels for pool breaks and naps.

- Some rides have "single rider" lines that are much shorter than the regular ones. Consider these whenever you can. Sure, you are not sitting next to your friend when you are on the ride, but that is only a few minutes of the day, and you can shave hours off of your total line waiting time.

- If you are going to Pleasure Island, consider hitting *Mannequins*, which has a no-kid policy on the weekends.

- Close down the park! Stay late and experience some smaller crowds, shorter lines, and fewer kids.

- Try the Richard Petty Driving Experience, a spa treatment, or a round of golf for a mostly child-free time.

- Avoid Moderate and Value resort food courts for dinner, and instead opt to dine at the Epcot World Showcase by doing the Snackapalooza taste sensation (see the "Snackapalooza" sidebar in Chapter 5, "Epcot: Bringing the World and the Future Together")!

- Consider carrying an iPod with multiple headphones that you can listen to together with your adult companions. It may drown out a temper tantrum going on in line ahead of you.

Nightlife

Read more about some of the nightlife activities at Downtown Disney and the BoardWalk in Chapter 8, "Disney After Dark: Downtown Disney and BoardWalk." These two sites offer some fun choices, but there are other places to go, too. Some of the resorts offer dining and lounge options that could match your needs, as well. Some of the best locales for nightlife on Disney property are

- Cool clubbing: Todd English's *bluezoo* in the Dolphin hotel

- Rowdy singing: *Jellyrolls* at the BoardWalk

- Dancing with a techno touch: *Mannequins* at Pleasure Island

- Sports Bar: *ESPN Zone* at the BoardWalk

- Dancing with an Art Deco touch: *Atlantic Dance Hall* at the BoardWalk

- Comedy: *The Comedy Warehouse* at Pleasure Island

tip If you don't see the nightlife you're looking for here, the Orlando area, particularly downtown and the International Drive strip, can bring more options your way.

Romance

The romantic dining spots and private getaways in Walt Disney World are numerous. Dining options cover the spectrum from formal elegance to cozy hideaway. Fireworks go off almost every night, giving you a great backdrop for a romantic dinner or evening stroll, and there are other activities and events that help set the mood, including private boating excursions, spa services, and opulent suites. Here are just some of the romantic options available at Walt Disney World:

- Dinner at *Victoria & Albert's* (formal), *California Grill* (casually elegant), *San Angel Inn* (cozy), or *Bongo's Cuban Café* (Miami/Caribbean casual elegance)
- Cocktails at Todd English's *bluezoo* (contemporary elegance)
- Dancing at *Atlantic Dance Hall*
- Private boating on the *Breathless,* a wood-paneled Chris Craft boat
- A nighttime walk along the BoardWalk
- Fireworks watching from your hotel room porch
- Walks along some of the secret paths at Animal Kingdom, or a quiet moment alone in some of the hidden grottos around Cinderella's Castle in the Magic Kingdom

Planning Special Events

Walt Disney World is a great place to celebrate a special event. As it is a popular destination for group events, sporting events, and honeymoons, it has an amazing array of facilities capable of handling most anything you may want to do. There are wedding pavilions next to the Grand Floridian Resort, convention facilities at several of the hotels, group dining facilities atop the National pavilions of the World Showcase at Epcot, sport fields at the Wide World of Sports complex, and boats that you can rent at most of the lagoons and other waterways. You can also plan large group gatherings via the Disney website by enrolling in the free Magical Gatherings program, which lets you plan with your friends online, even if you are coming from different cities. Since there are so many options, your best bet is to call 407-WDW-PLAY (407-939-7529), and let the friendly and knowledgeable staff help you with ideas and reservations.

Packing for Your Stay at Disney

Shorts, swimsuits, sunglasses, and sandals—that is all you need, right? *Wrong!* Make sure you take into account the low temperatures for the time of year when you are visiting, as a pair of slacks and maybe a sweater could transform an uncomfortably cold night into a perfect evening out. It is true that a sport coat and tie are basically unnecessary (unless you plan to dine at Victoria & Albert's), but some nice resort casual attire is required at a few restaurants and could make you feel better suited (no pun intended) at select restaurants and nightspots.

Other things you should consider packing?

- Keep a list of mail and email addresses handy, as well as stamps. First, to send postcards to friends and family, and also because some attractions have kiosks where you can send themed email postcards free of charge.
- Comfortable walking shoes for everyone!
- Snacks and beverages for the room, as well as for the days in the park.
- Sunscreen, lip balm, hats, sunglasses, ponchos, and bug spray.
- One autograph book per child, as well as a big pen (so that characters can grip them).
- Pool shoes for the water parks.
- Earplugs for kids who are scared by loud noises.
- Backpack or fanny pack for carrying necessities into the parks.
- Gum.

> **note** If you are shopping throughout Walt Disney World, keep an eye out for great scrapbooking supplies for the adults, and for the kids, take notice of the charm bracelet bars, where they can add a new charm at each park. Also, for the younger ones, think about the "build-your-own" Mr. Potato Head or My Little Pony stations where you can add special Disney-themed elements.

Time Savers

You'll find advice scattered throughout this book for shaving waiting time and making the most of your stay. The following sections offer you some up-front advice for saving time during your visit to WDW.

Using the FASTPASS Service

The FASTPASS is Disney's way of accelerating your fun! The FASTPASS service is available at the most popular rides, which are marked in this book with the FAST-PASS icon. What you do is get a ticket for an assigned time later in the day to ride the attraction. The line that you will get into is shorter than the traditional line, and in the meantime allows you to go do other things in the park. When you approach an attraction that has FASTPASS, you will see the traditional line, with a clock that estimates your wait. Off to the side will be the FASTPASS kiosks, with a clock displaying what time you will return to ride the attraction. Simply insert your park tickets

Book online at www.disneyworld.com

into one of the many kiosks, and you will get that ticket. Make sure you insert every ticket and get a FASTPASS for every member of your group. You can only have one FASTPASS at a time, so pick carefully. After you have come back and ridden the attraction (or after the time on the FASTPASS has expired), you are again eligible to get a FASTPASS at another attraction.

> **note** Don't forget to grab your ticket out of the FASTPASS kiosk. Leaving it behind can really be a hassle.

Rider Switch

As I said earlier, it is a fun vacation for everyone. Is there a thrill ride that you really want to try, but your child is too short to meet the height requirement? Not a problem. Get in line. When you get to the front, the first adult rides the attraction, while the second waits with the children. When the first is done, the children are passed to that adult, and the second adult rides the attraction. No need to wait in line twice or pass on the ride altogether.

> **tip** Go to the first ride that has FAST-PASS, get one, and then move on to the second ride. When you are done, you already have a "reserved" seat on the first ride in your pocket. Choose rides more toward to the back of the park, as many visitors get distracted by stores and attractions in the front of the park as they enter.

Extra Magic Hours

Available in both the mornings and the evenings, this program gives Disney resort guests exclusive access to the parks before or after normal operating hours. For the morning Extra Magic Hours, a park is open an hour earlier usual, but only to guests of Disney-owned resorts, as well as to guests from the Shades of Green hotel, the Swan and Dolphin, and the Hilton located on Hotel Plaza Boulevard. The evening version of Extra Magic Hours keeps a park open an extra three hours after normal closing times. Not all attractions are open at this time, but most of the popular ones are, so it is well worth getting in early or staying late to avoid some of the crowds. Check with the front desk for a schedule of what parks are opened early or stay open late.

E-Ride Nights

An infrequent but exclusive offer for guests of Disney-owned resorts, E-Ride Nights opens a park after normal operating hours for a limited number of visitors. You do have to pay to get in, but at a range of $10–15 per person, with only a few thousand other guests sharing the park with you, it is well worth it. Check with your hotel concierge to find out if there are any E-Ride Nights during your stay.

Disney vacation reservations: 1-407-939-7675

KNOW THE PARK HOURS

As with the Extra Magic Hours, park hours for each park do change throughout the year. You can always check ahead on the Walt Disney World website, where they usually post times for the next three months. It is important to do so, as occasionally a park will be rented out for a special event and can to close early. This can help you plan your days and avoid the disappointment of having to leave a park earlier than expected. Typical operating times are

Magic Kingdom: Opens at 9 a.m., closes at 6 p.m.

Epcot Future World: Opens at 9 a.m., closes at 7 p.m.

Epcot World Showcase: Opens at 11 a.m., closes at 9 p.m.

Disney-MGM: Opens at 9 a.m., closes at 9 p.m.

Animal Kingdom: Opens at 9 a.m., closes at 5 p.m.

Water Parks: Open at 10 a.m., close at 6 p.m.

Disney Guest Services

ATMs

They are everywhere, so you should have no problem finding one. Every resort and park has at least one.

Baby Care Centers

These centers are located in each park, including both water parks as well as Downtown Disney. These are great for changing or feeding a baby.

Baby Sitting

In-room baby sitting is available, known as *Kid's Night Out*. Call 407-828-0920 for reservations. Guess what; they don't just baby-sit! They can actually take the kids out to attractions if you want them to. Typically, rates run around $14 per hour for one child, and additional kids are just a couple dollars more per hour added to that.

Childcare

Many of the deluxe resort hotels at Disney have *Children's Activity Centers* for kids aged 4 to 12. These provide an ideal way for you to keep the kids entertained while

Book online at www.disneyworld.com

you get an adult's night out. They get dinner, movies, activities, and fun. Make reservations by way of calling 407-WDW-DINE (407-939-3463). No, you do not have to be a guest of the actual hotel for your kid to enroll. Also of special note are three kids' programs at the Grand Floridian. These activities include the *Grand Adventure in Cooking*, the *Wonderland Tea Party*, and the *Disney's Pirate Adventure*. These are all for kids aged 4–10. Usually you are going to have to pay about $10 per hour, per child, and reservations are necessary.

Kennels

There are five kennels located at Walt Disney World, with one near the entrance to each park and at the check-in area for the Fort Wilderness Resort and Campground. These air-conditioned kennels are members of the American Boarding Kennel Association. Costs are $6 a day or $9 a night if you are a resort guest, and you are required to visit your pet daily. Reservations are required.

Lockers

Lockers are available at all of the theme parks, the water parks, and Downtown Disney. There is a nominal fee, but it can be worth it, especially if you are carrying a large supply of baby supplies or swim stuff for a water park visit later in the day.

Shipping Packages to Rooms

This is a *tremendous* program, and one that will make your life a bit less hectic. If you are staying at a Disney-owned hotel resort, you can have any purchases made at a Disney park, Downtown Disney, or the BoardWalk shipped to your hotel room. You have to give it a day to get there, but it is great if you find the perfect gift early in the morning but don't want to carry it around all day long.

Strollers

You can rent strollers at each of the parks for $7 per day ($8 charge with a $1 refund when you return the stroller). Doubles are available for around $13 dollars. The strollers are durable and large-wheeled, have plenty of storage areas, and have signs with your name on them so that you can find them if you have parked them outside of a show along with the hundreds of others of parents. If you rent in one park, you get a stroller in any other park that same day at no charge. There is also a length-of-stay rental available.

Travelers with Disabilities

All Disney resort hotels offer facilities for guest with disabilities. You can find out more by clicking on the "Guests with Disabilities" link on the home page of www.disneyworld.com, or by calling 407-939-7807. For TTY connections, call 407-939-7670.

> **tip** In your collection of Trip Cards is a listing of some of the important numbers that you need to have on hand for a variety of reasons, such as getting a babysitter, reserving a seat for dinner, or making changes to your reservation.

Medical

If you have a medical emergency, contact any Disney staffer and they will help you find the fastest and most appropriate care required. There are a number of facilities in the immediate area, so if you expect a possible need, make sure you discuss it with your hotel desk staff upon your arrival.

Do Ahead Checklist

You have now planned out the basics of your trip. So what do you really need to do before you leave? Tick the items off this checklist as you wrap them up:

- Set budget
- Airline tickets ordered (if applicable)
- Hotel reservations made
- Park Tickets ordered
- Golf, spa, or other special activity reservations made
- Event tickets, such as Cirque du Soleil ordered
- Daily park schedule planned
- Daily dining plan scheduled
- Meal reservations made
- Childcare reservations made
- Transportation to/from airport reserved
- Park information review
- Trip Cards filled out
- Packing list planned out

Summary

Okay, you have planned out the big things. Tickets, travel, time of visit, and the big one: *budget*! Well that takes care of the "chores" associated with this trip. Now comes the fun part! Let's start by picking what hotel is going to be your home during the Disney extravaganza. Are you staying in a Polynesian paradise or in a Caribbean retreat? Perhaps you will stay in a hotel dedicated to all the cool trends of the last century? Decisions, decisions!

Choosing a Hotel: Leisure Rules!

Where you stay is as important as what parks you visit, what rides you go on, and where you eat. The right hotel can make the vacation perfect, and the wrong one can ruin it. This chapter is going to help you pick the right hotel, taking into consideration your unique vacation needs, the location that best suits your plans, and—most importantly—your budget!

Of course there are literally thousands of hotels in the greater Orlando area, so covering them all here is out of the question. What you will find is an overview of several of the best options for someone who is going to Walt Disney World. Most of the hotels previewed are on-property accommodations, which are located on the grounds of Walt Disney World. There are also a few hotels shown here that are not run by Disney, to show you a sampling of what else is available.

In this chapter:

* Review hotels to select which best meet your budget and needs
* Learn about the difference between staying on- and off-property
* Review hotel features to get the most out of your travel dollar

To do list

❑ Determine if you want to stay at an on- or off-property hotel

❑ Select the hotel classification that best suits your budget

❑ Pick your hotel, and learn the best ways to save on making a reservation

Choosing Your Hotel

So with so many hotel choices, how do you go about deciding where to stay? You can choose your hotel in just a few simple steps.

Things You'll Need

❑ Your Trip Card

❑ Pen or pencil and paper

Step 1: Decide If You Should Stay On- or Off-property

With a few exceptions, "on-property" means staying at a WDW-owned and operated hotel. It used to be that Disney only offered a few hotel choices of their own, and they were all pretty expensive. But since the introduction of Moderate and Value class hotels (with rates as low as $49 a night during the slower times of the year), you can stay on-property as affordably as you can off-property.

So which should you choose? Well, if your vacation includes a lot of non-WDW activities (like other theme parks), staying off-property may make your morning and evening commutes a bit shorter. If, however, you are just hitting Disney parks, you are probably better served sticking to a Disney hotel. The perks that you get for staying at a Disney hotel make your investment there a better choice. Staying at an on-property hotel gives you these benefits that regular visitors do not get:

- **Extra Magic Hours** access at select parks lets Disney Resort guests (and *only* Disney Resort Guests!) into those parks an hour early or lets them stay after standard closing for up to three hours. Ask what parks have Magic Hours during your stay when you check in.

- Transportation throughout Walt Disney World by bus, water launch, or monorail is free.

- **Magical Express Service** provides a pickup service at the Orlando International Airport, complete with baggage pickup and handling, as well as transportation to the resort and back to the airport at the end of your vacation (these services are not available to guests of the Disney Swan and Disney Dolphin resorts.)

- Children services including in-room babysitting, activity centers, and dinner clubs (varies by hotel) give you an extra set of hands to watch the kids, at a charge of course!
- Exclusive access to E-Ride nights
- You can charge purchases to your room.
- You can have purchases in the parks shipped to your room.

Most visitors agree that the Disney resorts are the best choice, now that there is a full range of budget alternatives. The majority of this chapter, therefore, is devoted to in-depth reviews of Disney hotels and resorts. In "Off-Property Hotel Choices," later in this chapter, I offer some great ideas for choosing from among the hundreds of other hotels in the Orlando area, and finding great deals at hotels with Disney-affiliated discounts.

Step 2: Create a "Short List" of Hotels That Match Your Budget

After reading Chapter 1, "Planning your Walt Disney World Trip," you should have an idea of what you have in your hotel budget. So with that figure—and the dates you'll be visiting—in mind, you can create a short list of hotel options.

If you're planning to stay in a Disney hotel, check your options on Table 2.1. Find those hotels that meet your budget by looking at the range of rates available for the dates when you would be visiting Walt Disney World. If you choose in step 1 to stay at a non-Disney hotel, you can get some ideas of where to start searching for hotels that match your budget in "Off-Property Hotel Choices," later in this chapter.

Step 3: Pick Your Hotel

Okay, now you should have a short list of hotel choices. The next step is to read the reviews listed here, and then rank your choices in order of preference. In each review, I list the hotel's location, the transportation options it offers to other areas of the park, and any special features the hotel offers. Beyond price, these are some of the most important considerations when choosing a Disney hotel.

Don't limit yourself to a single choice. Orlando hotels sell out more often than you might imagine, so keep those second and third choices handy. Especially if you are booking

note Want to check out these hotels? Visit **www.disneyworld.com**, and select "Resorts" from the upper-left menu. If you want to call for reservations, just dial 407-WDW-MAGIC (939.6244), but before doing that, check out Chapter 1, and make sure that you have considered some of the money-saving packages.

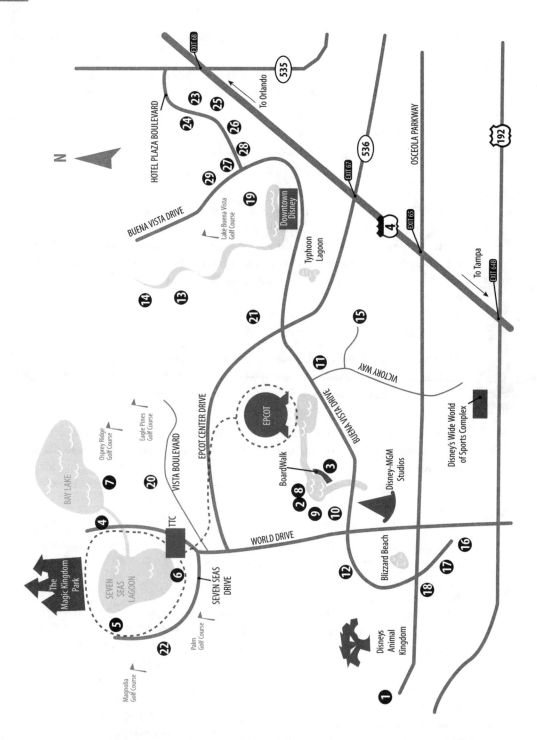

See Table 2.1 for map of Disney hotel listings. See page 58 for non-Disney hotel listings.

tickets and hotel via the Disney website, you need to be ready to switch to a different choice, as there may be a slightly better deal on one of these alternative selections.

For a quick comparison of hotel rates, see Table 2.1; it lists Disney's hotels, their seasons, and rates. These dates and rates are accurate as of the writing of this book, but they can change; you can call or visit the hotel's website to get current rates when you're ready to make a final choice.

Table 2.1 Disney Hotel Rates Throughout the Year

Hotel	Value Season	Regular Season	Peak Season	Holiday Season
Deluxe Hotels Season Dates	Jan 1–Feb 16 Jul 5–Oct 4 Nov 27–Dec 19	Apr 17–Jul 4 Oct 4–Nov 26	Feb 17–Apr 16	Dec 20–31
Deluxe Hotels				
❶ Disney's Animal Kingdom Lodge	$199–$340	$239–$385	$289–$445	$324–$510
❷ Disney's Beach Club Resort	$294–$465	$334–$525	$404–$595	$459–$660
❸ Disney's BoardWalk Inn	$294–$560	$334–$615	$404–$690	$459–$800
❹ Disney's Contemporary Resort	$244–$310	$274–$350	$319–$400	$359–$440
❺ Disney's Grand Floridian Resort & Spa	$349–$430	$394–$490	$459–$580	$534–$645
❻ Disney's Polynesian Resort	$304–$400	$354–$445	$419–$520	$484–$580
❼ Disney's Wilderness Lodge	$199–$400	$239–$450	$289–$515	$324–$560
❽ Disney's Yacht Club Resort	$294–$355	$334–$405	$404–$470	$459–$525
❾ Walt Disney World Dolphin*	$259–$339	n/a	$289–$379	n/a
❿ Walt Disney World Swan*	$259–$339	n/a	$289–$379	n/a
Moderate and Value Resorts Season Dates	Jan 1–Feb 16 Aug 28–Oct 4 Nov 27–Dec 19	Apr 17–Aug 27 Oct 5–Nov 26	Feb 17–Apr 16	Dec 20–31
Moderate Hotels				
⓫ Disney's Caribbean Beach Resort	$134–$149	$149–$165	$169–$194	$184–$209
⓬ Disney's Coronado Springs Resort	$134–$149	$149–$165	$169–$194	$184–$209
⓭ Disney's Port Orleans Resort French Quarter	$134–$149	$149–$165	$169–$194	$184–$209
⓮ Disney's Port Orleans Resort Riverside	$134–$149	$149–$165	$169–$194	$184–$209
Value Hotels				
⓯ Disney's Pop Century Resort	$77–$89	$99–$111	$109–$121	$119–$131
⓰ Disney's All-Star Movies Resort	$77–$89	$99–$111	$109–$121	$119–$131
⓱ Disney's All-Star Music Resort	$77–$89	$99–$111	$109–$121	$119–$131
⓲ Disney's All-Star Sports Resort	$77–$89	$99–$111	$109–$121	$119–$131

Hotel	Value Season	Regular Season	Peak Season	Holiday Season
Home away from Home Hotels (follow same rate season as Deluxe Resorts)				
❷ Disney's Beach Club Villas	$294	$334	$404	$459
❸ Disney's BoardWalk Villas	$294	$334	$404	$459
⓴ Disney's Fort Wilderness Resort & Campground	See the review for the many camping options available.			
⓳ Disney's Saratoga Springs Resort & Spa	$259	$289	$339	$379
㉑ Disney's Old Key West Resort	$259	$289	$339	$379
❼ The Villas at Disney's Wilderness Lodge	$289	$324	$389	$499
Other Hotels				
㉒ Shades of Green	Rates vary by Military Classification			

*The Walt Disney World Dolphin and the Walt Disney World Swan have two rate seasons, unlike other Disney hotels. Their seasons for 2005, for example, are as follows: Value: Jan 1–15, May 1—December 20; Peak: January 16—April 30, December 21–December 31.

MUST-STAY RESORTS AT WDW

Here are my personal picks for great places to stay in or near Walt Disney World. I've chosen one for each category included in this chapter:

Favorite Deluxe Resort: Wilderness Lodge

The least expensive of all the Deluxe hotels, the soaring lobby alone is worth a visit.

Favorite Moderate Resort: Port Orleans Resort Riverside

Great amenities and boat access to Downtown Disney, when other Moderate hotels get you there by bus.

Favorite Value Resort: Pop Century Resort

The newest Value resort, and in an area of its own, so less of the congestion that other Value resorts experience.

Favorite Home Away from Home Resort: Disney BoardWalk Villas

Staying at a Home Away from Home Resort usually means you have a large group, and having somewhere nearby (such as the BoardWalk!) where they can get some entertainment, as well as some basic convenience shopping, makes the stay *much* better for everyone.

Favorite Off-Property Hotel: Gaylord Palms

The dome-covered interior with various Florida-themed areas, including a Spanish colonial castle, keep your kids saying *wow*, even after they are out of the parks!

Deluxe Hotels at Walt Disney World

Okay, let's start at the top, and work our way down. The Deluxe hotels at Walt Disney World offer you the largest rooms, the best locations, and a variety of amenities to make your stay comfortable. They have room service, kids' programs, and the most convenient transportation to the parks and other locations. The prices are understandably more expensive than at the Moderate and Value hotels, but deals can be had, and even if you pay full price you may find that your hotel plays a role in a great vacation experience.

Now, just because you may be paying top dollar for these rooms, don't expect excessive luxury. Two identical rooms in New York City and Des Moines, Iowa would charge different rates because of their locations. Similarly the rooms at these resorts may offer little more than a standard hotel room in your home town, but remember that the extra charge here is based on getting other kinds of benefits for your money. First, you get a lot more hotel-based amenities than the other resorts, as mentioned previously. Second, in most cases, you are closer to the parks than the less-expensive resorts, either by being a walk, a boat trip, or a monorail ride away from at least one theme park. Finally, the rooms are larger than those at the other resorts, which any family on a trip will tell you can make all the difference. It all comes down to what you want out of the vacation, and what you can afford. In the case of the Deluxe resorts, if you have the means, they are worth the money.

note Again, all rates listed here are accurate as of the time of this writing, but are subject to change.

❶ Disney's Animal Kingdom Lodge

Location: Animal Kingdom Area

Price Range: $199–$510

Transportation: Bus to all theme parks, water parks, nightlife areas, and transportation center.

Special Features: Wildlife preserve view from select rooms, morning safari tours through preserve (additional cost applies, reservations required), as well as a spa on site.

The newest of the Deluxe hotels, the Lodge is obviously closely aligned to the Animal Kingdom Park. The lobby is intended to make you feel like you are in an African safari lodge, and the décor throughout carries that feeling, including open pit fires for storytelling and informal gatherings. This hotel offers some unique African-themed dining, but lunchtime options are limited.

tip Select rooms in the Animal Kingdom Lodge have a view of a savannah-like holding area for animals from the park, but at a price. Before you spend the extra money for one of these views, ask yourself how much time you plan to spend lounging in the room, and remember that you can see this wildlife area from some viewing areas around the hotel.

❷ Disney's Beach Club Resort

Location: Epcot Area

Price Range: $294–$660

Transportation: Walk or boat to BoardWalk and Epcot, boat to MGM, bus to all other theme parks, water parks, Downtown Disney, and transportation center.

Special Features: The best pool system at WDW. The great location gets you quickly to MGM and Epcot as well as the BoardWalk, but away from the nighttime noise that can occur on the BoardWalk.

The Beach Club is paired with the Yacht Club, sharing the best pools at WDW. It actually has three pools, including a lazy river for drifting on inner tubes, an active pool, and a quiet pool that has a sandy beach entrance. The Beach Club has a more relaxed atmosphere than the Yacht Club, but still delivers an upscale experience. It is probably the more kid-friendly of the two, complete with the Cape May Café, a buffet restaurant that features a character breakfast. This can be a nice excuse for your kids to sleep in and re-energize before hitting the parks.

TAKE A POOL BREAK!

There is no greater service that the Resorts at Walt Disney World provide to families with children than their pools. Any group with children should include afternoon breaks to their hotel pool as a way to keep their kids relaxed and happy. You are never going to see it all, so make the time you have about enjoying yourself, not chasing from ride to ride. And a special bonus: If you are staying at a Disney Resort, you are allowed to use almost all of the pools at the other Disney resorts, even if you are not staying there. What other pools should you try to visit? Try these popular hits:

- ✳ BoardWalk Inn. You will love the slide!
- ✳ Wilderness Lodge. Geysers and a camp theme make the views part of the fun.
- ✳ Yacht and Beach Clubs. The lazy river and grounded ship make for a fun pool for adults as well as kids.
- ✳ Coronado Springs. Probably not that special of a pool, but the towering pyramid adds an exotic atmosphere.
- ✳ Honorary Mention: Value Hotel Pools. If you think that your pool is not as good as the ones at the more expensive hotels, think again. These pools are generally newer, and the convenience of having them outside your room instead of a bus ride away makes them your best choice.

❸ Disney's BoardWalk Inn

Location: Epcot Area

Price Range: $294–$800

Transportation: Walk or boat to Epcot park, walk or boat to MGM, bus to all other theme parks, water parks, Downtown Disney, and transportation center.

Special Features: Immediate access to the BoardWalk, and all the restaurants and fun that they offer. Larger-than-average rooms.

Let your family be transported back to an 1800s-era Atlantic seaboard resort at this ideal hotel location. One of our favorites at Disney, the hotel's nostalgic interior provides the charm, but the location makes it a top choice. You can walk to Epcot or boat to MGM, and you have the BoardWalk entertainment strip just an elevator ride away. You're paying for the location, here; the rooms themselves aren't anything special. They are larger than most other rooms at WDW, however, which matters when you have a lot of luggage and shopping bags.

❹ Disney's Contemporary Resort

Location: Magic Kingdom Area

Price Range: $244–$440

Transportation: Monorail to Magic Kingdom, and Epcot via the transportation center bus to all other theme parks, water parks, nightlife areas, and transportation center.

Special Features: Indoor monorail stop, so you stay cool waiting for the coolest transportation at WDW, while others sit out in the heat waiting for a bus.

How do you design a hotel and have it still look cutting-edge decades later? Have a monorail run through it! The hotel may not have a warm and cozy feel to it, but the stores are better than at most, the buffet restaurant is a great place for character meals with kids, and the *California Grill* at the top of the hotel is our #1 favorite restaurant, both for the food and the view. And be honest, while it is convenient that you are feet away from a monorail that can get you to the Magic Kingdom in seconds, the real appeal is that you have it running through the building. It just never gets old!

❺ Disney's Grand Floridian Resort & Spa

Location: Magic Kingdom Area

Price Range: $349–$645

Transportation: Monorail to Magic Kingdom, and Epcot via the transportation center bus to all other theme parks, water parks, nightlife areas, and transportation center.

Special Features: An onsite spa, a pool for the exclusive use of this resort's guests, and a monorail stop are just a few of the amenities that make you feel as high-class as the high-end room rates.

This is the most luxurious hotel at WDW, with the high-end selection of shops, restaurants, and lounges that you would come to expect. The Grand Floridian is without question the most exclusive hotel at WDW, and the most expensive. The interior is designed with an elegant southern charm, though it can be a bit sterile and cold. The shopping is very high end, and the hotel is also the home of the most upscale restaurant at WDW, *Victoria and Albert's*. The lounges offer some nice romantic, intimate nooks as well. Despite having a monorail stop and great kid activity programs, this hotel's atmosphere doesn't feel especially kid friendly.

❻ Disney's Polynesian Resort

Location: Magic Kingdom Area

Price Range: $304–$580

Transportation: Monorail to Magic Kingdom, and Epcot via the transportation center, bus to all other theme parks, water parks, nightlife areas, and transportation center.

Special Features: A monorail stop and one of the most popular entertainment shows (the *Spirit of Aloha Dinner* show) in WDW.

One of the original hotels at WDW, the south pacific theme can really *wow* kids and make them know they are somewhere special. Despite its age, constant updates make this resort a great place to stay. The quick monorail ride to the Magic Kingdom and the Transportation and Ticket Center, along with the longtime popular luau show and newer *Ohana* dining experiences make this an ideal hotel for families with kids. But don't expect too much updated luxury. If you are torn between this and another deluxe resort, where price and everything else is even, you might opt for one of the newer alternatives.

❼ Disney's Wilderness Lodge

Location: Magic Kingdom Area

Price Range: $199–$560

Transportation: Boat to the Magic Kingdom, bus to all other theme parks, water parks, nightlife areas, and transportation center.

> **tip** If you are considering a moderate level hotel, at least check the Wilderness Lodge prices first. You might be able to upgrade your vacation experience for little extra cash.

Special Features: A lobby that will take your breath away, man-made geysers, crafts by the pool, and the least expensive Deluxe-class rooms.

Designed in the spirit of the large National Park Lodges of the Western United States, the Wilderness Lodge greets you with a cavernous lobby that is alive with western log cabin warmth. Amenities include one of the best fine restaurants (*Artist's Point*), and perhaps the best non-character restaurant experience for kids (*Whispering Canyon Cafe*), where the food is good, and the fun is better. The Lodge sports some of the least expensive Deluxe-level hotel rooms, while still only being a boat ride away from the Magic Kingdom.

❽ Disney's Yacht Club Resort

Location: Epcot Area

Price Range: $294–$525

Transportation: Walk or boat to BoardWalk and Epcot, boat to MGM, bus to all other theme parks, water parks, Downtown Disney, and transportation center.

Special Features: The best pool systems at WDW. The great location gets you quickly to MGM and Epcot as well as the BoardWalk, but away from the noise from nighttime crowds at the BoardWalk.

Paired with the Beach Club, the Yacht Club shares many facilities, such as the great pools, but has a more upscale atmosphere. The upper-crust New England experience really makes you feel like you are at a resort worthy of the cost of your room, and the location is a major plus, due to the proximity to parks and the BoardWalk. Of the Disney hotels located on the lagoon at the BoardWalk, this is the best choice, based on elegant hotel décor and facilities.

❾ Walt Disney World Dolphin

Location: Epcot Area

Price Range: $259–$379

Transportation: Walk or boat to BoardWalk and Epcot park, boat to MGM, bus to all other theme parks, water parks, Downtown Disney, and transportation center.

Special Features: The Dolphin has a National rental car desk, and if you are a Starwood Points member, you can earn points on your stay.

The Dolphin is one of a pair of Michael Graves-designed hotels near the BoardWalk (the Swan being the other) that are hard to miss with their teal and orange color schemes and gigantic sculptures on top. The hotel is actually run by Sheraton, but guests receive most of the same perks as a Disney World Resort guest. The Dolphin has a great steakhouse (Shula's), a hot new trendy restaurant

note Note that the Swan and Dolphin's guests do not get the Magical Express Service from the airport, and they cannot charge purchases in the parks to their room as with other Disney resorts, which is a bigger disappointment than you might think. The Dolphin also hosts numerous conventions throughout the year, and uses different dates for their rate seasons.

(bluezoo), a fair cafeteria, and a fun beach/pool area that they share with the Swan. The location within walking distance of Epcot and the BoardWalk make it a great hotel choice for families, though it is not as Mickey Mouse-heavy in its décor as some kids might prefer.

⑩ Walt Disney World Swan

Location: Epcot Area

Price Range: $259–$379

Transportation: Walk or boat to BoardWalk and Epcot park, boat to MGM, bus to all other theme parks, water parks, Downtown Disney, and transportation center.

Special Features: The Westin Heavenly Bed is the most relaxing sleep that you will get at WDW, and you can earn Starwood points on your stay at the Swan.

A sister hotel to the Dolphin, the Swan is run by Westin hotels, a Starwood chain (just like Sheraton). As with the Dolphin, guests here receive most of the same benefits as a Disney resort guest, with the noticeable exceptions being that you can't charge things to your room, and you don't get the Magical Express Service. Each room features the Westin Heavenly Bed which, believe me, is worth the price of admission. The Swan is an adult-friendly hotel, with a subdued décor, but don't think kids aren't welcome here. The Swan shares pool/beach facilities with the Dolphin, and there is a restaurant that has a regular character dinner, though it is not one of the better character meal experiences at WDW. Unlike the Dolphin, the convention business is less significant here, though they too follow a different set of dates for the rate seasons.

caution A former favorite, the Swan's poor customer service has notched it down a bit, though the beds and location still make it a good choice.

Moderate Hotels at Walt Disney World

The Moderate hotels at Walt Disney World are a great alternative to the deluxe hotels, saving you around $100 a day, without much loss of amenities. The rooms are a bit smaller than most rooms in the Deluxe category, but they are far from cramped. Probably the most significant trade-off for saving some money is in the transportation options. Where most Deluxe hotels offer a monorail ride, boat trip, or short walk to one or two theme parks, when you stay at a Moderate hotel, you'll have to join the bus circuit every morning to get to the theme parks. But don't think that riding the bus means you're slumming. Disney is reported to have the largest fleet of buses in the world, so the waits are not so bad, and the buses are well maintained, clean, and comfortable. Limited room service is available (usually just pizza from 4 to 11 p.m.), childcare and babysitting services are offered, and they all have laundry facilities. Consider these resorts seriously, as deals can often make them fit in your budget.

⑪ Disney's Caribbean Beach Resort

Location: Epcot Area

Price Range: $134–$209

Transportation: Bus to all theme parks, water parks, nightlife areas, and transportation center.

Special Features: The largest rooms in the Moderate class and a great central location to all of Walt Disney World.

The Caribbean feel is relaxed and somewhat toned down. This is a fine moderate priced hotel, but there is nothing special here to distinguish it from the others.

SHOP THE HOTELS

Every hotel has its own stores with sundries and logo-laden apparel. But you will find that the selection of clothes, toys, and other collectibles is significantly greater at the parks and nightlife districts. So what should you consider buying here? Here are some suggestions:

❋ Need batteries for the camera? Don't wait until you are in the park if you know you need some; get them here where there are no lines. Of course prices are pretty steep, so if you can plan ahead and bring them with you from home, all the better.

❋ Autograph books. If your children are going to be getting character signatures, have the book, and a good pen with a fatter handle (so that the character can hold onto it easily) ready before you set off to the first park. You never know when you will see their favorite personality, and you don't want them to miss the opportunity because you were waiting to buy an autograph book in one of the parks.

❋ Postcards and stamps. If you planned on sending a hello to the jealous ones back home, get it done right away, so that you don't forget.

⑫ Disney's Coronado Springs Resort

Location: Animal Kingdom Area

Price Range: $134–$209

Transportation: Bus to all theme parks, water parks, nightlife areas, and transportation center.

Special Features: Health Club, business services and facilities, wireless access, and a barbershop.

Coronado Springs is becoming a more active convention site, so the crowd here may seem less like a traditional Disney crowd than you might imagine. The good news is that if your timing is right and there is a big convention underway, you might find buses to the parks in the morning lighter, as most of the attendees might just be heading to the meeting rooms! Enjoy the décor of the southwest and Mexico, complete with a pyramid at poolside that adds a somewhat elegant feel to the area.

⑬⑭ Disney's Port Orleans Resort

Location: Downtown Disney Area

Price Range: $134–$209

Transportation: Boat to Downtown Disney, and bus to all other theme parks, water parks, BoardWalk, and transportation center.

Special Features: Boat Service to Downtown Disney.

The Port Orleans resort is split into two sections, each with its own hotel; the French Quarter offers the southern charm of New Orleans, while the larger Riverside section has a Mississippi River-country feel.

> **tip** The hotels in both sections of the Port Orleans Resort are the best choices of all the moderate hotels due to their boat service to Downtown Disney.

The French Quarter has both a lounge and a food court, but no full-service restaurant. The atmosphere is fun, but somewhat elegant, and might be the better choice for an all-adult group staying in the Port Orleans Resort, as long as the full-service restaurant's location in the Riverside section is not an issue.

The Riverside area of Port Orleans has a Mark Twain-era, southern river country décor. The outdoor atmosphere is fun and nostalgic, and it gives you a reason to stick around and experience the relaxed mood of the south. I would recommend it over the French Quarter half of the Port Orleans Resort simply due to the closeness of the amenities.

Value Hotels at Walt Disney World

Everyone who is not independently wealthy should shout a big *hooray* for the Disney Value Hotels! While it may have taken Disney a while to get the hint that we needed some more affordable hotel options, they certainly did it right from the very beginning.

The Value hotels may have smaller rooms, no table service restaurants, and no monorail stops, but Disney does not treat guests at these hotels like third-class citizens. The hotels are decorated with a enthusiastic sense of fun and whimsy, complete with three-story football helmets, saxophones, and Rubik's cubes. They all sport fun food courts that will take care of your food needs, and keep you within your budget. The pools are basic, but set in a fun environment, certainly up to your kid's standards and expectations. The hotels all have in-room pizza delivery, laundry facilities, and childcare and babysitting services. These hotels are designed to make family vacations affordable, so Disney really hit the mark.

caution About the only caution I'd offer for the Value hotels is to those adults who want to avoid kids: These hotels aren't good places to do that. Most guests come as families, and the lack of lounges leaves you no child-free havens to escape the little tikes.

Except for their décor, these hotels are all pretty similar. Beyond that, the only deciding factor when choosing among them will be the deals they're offering when you're ready to travel. Therefore, the "Special Features" for each of these hotels is "Price, Price, Price! "

⑮ Disney's Pop Century Resort

Location: Epcot Area

Price Range: $77–$131

Transportation: Bus to all theme parks, water parks, nightlife areas, and transportation center.

caution Parking issues at Pop Century have been reported, as you may end up hiking from your car to your room. If you are driving, perhaps another Value resort would be a better choice.

Three-story-tall Rubik's cubes and big wheels set the tone for this resort that pays homage to many of the popular toys, fashions, and trends of the twentieth century. This is the newest of all Value resorts, so it is in the best shape. Also, this resort is set off by itself, away from the other Value resorts, so it can on occasion have a little less congestion, both on the grounds and on the transport buses. For that reason, it serves as the recommended choice in the Value class, though only if there is not a lower-price alternative among the other three choices.

⑯ Disney's All-Star Movies Resort

Location: Animal Kingdom Area

Price Range: $77–$131

Transportation Bus to all theme parks, water parks, nightlife areas, and transportation center.

Disney movie characters decorate the resort grounds, including Goofy, Mickey, and a few newer ones, like from the Mighty Ducks. Not as many of the newer movie characters are shown here, but the grounds are still colorful and fun.

note Disney-owned resort rooms have a great TV feature. Every evening there are bedtime stories told by Disney characters on the park channel.

17 Disney's All-Star Music Resort

Location: Animal Kingdom Area

Price Range: $77–$131

Transportation: Bus to all theme parks, water parks, nightlife areas, and transportation center.

Jazz, country, and rock and roll are the themes of the grounds, complete with massive cowboy boots, drum sets, and 10-foot tall musical notes. It is perhaps the least colorful of the Value resorts, but by no means ugly or boring.

18 Disney's All-Star Sports Resort

Location: Animal Kingdom Area

Price Range: $77–$131

Transportation: Bus to all theme parks, water parks, nightlife areas, and transportation center.

This is probably the best-decorated Value resort. The gigantic basketballs, football helmets, cheerleading megaphones, and other sports items are going to make any little boy or girl let out a big "wow."

Home Away from Home Hotels a Walt Disney World

But you have a big group? Okay, let's move on from these traditional hotel rooms to something a bit more industrial strength!

Accommodations in the "Home Away from Home" category offer you larger spaces for larger groups. Studios as well as 1- and 2-bedroom villas are available, and the choices go on from there. Many of these are also Disney Vacation Club Resort properties, a timeshare program that offers resort hotels throughout Walt Disney World, as well as at

note Disney has gotten into the timeshare business, just like many other companies. Throughout Walt Disney World, you will find information podiums dedicated to luring you in to one of their sales presentations. If timeshares are of interest to you, you should know that their properties are not just at Walt Disney World. They also have beachfront resort properties in Vero Beach, FL, and Hilton Head, SC, and there are packages that can include these other resorts. To find out more, visit www.disneyvacationclub.com.

other locations throughout the U.S. (see note in this chapter). Perhaps the most important benefit for the majority of the accommodations offered here are the in-room kitchenettes. Not only is it convenient to have some of the features available in your room, but if you can genuinely expect to eat a few meals there, you are going to dramatically reduce your vacation cost. Some of these choices are connected to resorts we have already reviewed in this chapter, so you should already have an idea of what the atmosphere and location are like. But if you need a bit more than the average hotel room can offer, these could be the right solution for you!

⑲ Disney's Saratoga Springs Resort & Spa

Location: Downtown Disney Area

Price Range: $259–$379

Transportation: Boat or walk to Downtown Disney, bus to all theme parks, water parks, the BoardWalk, and transportation center.

Special Features: The newest resort at WDW, within walking distance to Downtown Disney, makes it a great location for those adult groups planning on nightly clubbing at Pleasure Island".

One of the Disney Vacation Club properties, Saratoga Springs transports you to the refined world of upstate New York horse racing. The atmosphere here is more sub-dued and quiet than at other resorts, though not unfriendly to families. You can select from a studio, or from one-, two-, or three-bedroom villas. The view across the lagoon of Pleasure Island provides a nighttime show that you can enjoy from your porch.

❷ Disney's Beach Club Villas

Location: Epcot Area

Price Range: $294–459

Transportation: Walk or boat to BoardWalk and Epcot, boat to MGM, bus to all other theme parks, water parks, Downtown Disney, and transportation center.

Special Features: The best pool systems at WDW. The great location gets you quickly to MGM and Epcot as well as the BoardWalk, providing nighttime entertainment and dining for the whole family.

Attached to the Disney Beach Club Resort, studios can handle up to four guests, with an added crib if requested. The rooms have a queen bed and a double size sleeper sofa, as well as a kitchenette. Villas can handle as many as eight guests, dependent upon the rooms' configuration. This is one of the Disney Vacation Club resorts.

note See the Beach Club Resort listing for more information on the dining and recreation in the area.

❸ Disney's BoardWalk Villas

Location: Epcot Area

Price Range: $294–459

Transportation: Walk or boat to Epcot park, boat to MGM, bus to all other theme parks, water parks, Downtown Disney, and transportation center.

Special Features: The BoardWalk is at your hotel, so fun for the whole family is right outside your door.

The villas are a great large-family option, holding up to eight guests and a crib. The smaller four-guest studios are nice too, and like the villas, have kitchenettes. The resort décor and facilities are shared with the Disney BoardWalk Inn, providing you a bright and festive escape to a late-nineteenth century Atlantic seaboard resort. This is one of the Disney Vacation Club resorts.

⓴ Disney's Fort Wilderness Resort & Campground

Location: Magic Kingdom Area

Price Range: $38–$339

Transportation: Boat to Magic Kingdom, bus to all other theme parks, water parks, nightlife areas, and transportation center.

Special Features: Genuinely different accommodations from all others at Walt Disney World, giving you an outdoor, camping-style experience without having to hike too much.

Get close to nature, but not too close! The selection of accommodations here are truly different than at any other Disney resort. From campsites that will cost you less than $40, to rustic cabins that hold six, the range of options are significant. The campsites can include electricity, water, sewer, and cable, where the cabins include kitchen facilities, a dining table big enough for four, and a lot of other "non-roughing it" amenities, such as cable TV, air conditioning, and daily housekeeping. There is also a charcoal grill, so you can cook out in the great outdoors after a long day at the parks!

For campers, nearby comfort stations have air conditioning to save you in the height of summer, as well as private showers, laundry facilities, restrooms, and ice machines. These sites are reported to hold as many as 10.

㉑ Disney's Old Key West Resort

Location: Downtown Disney Area

Price Range: $259–$379

Transportation: Boat to Downtown Disney, bus to all theme parks, water parks, BoardWalk, and transportation center.

Special Features: The boat to Downtown Disney makes getting to shopping and entertainment fast and easy.

The island feel of the resort is relaxing, and the studios and villas offer pretty much the same thing as most of the other resorts in this class. While there seems to be nothing to distinguish this resort from others, it is a pleasant atmosphere that seems more natural in the Florida location, so if you want the Disney theming toned down, this is the place to stay. It is yet another good location for adult groups, due to the proximity to Downtown Disney and Pleasure Island. This is one of the Disney Vacation Club resorts.

❼ The Villas at Disney's Wilderness Lodge

Location: Magic Kingdom Area

Price Range: $289–$499

Transportation: Boat to the Magic Kingdom, bus to all other theme parks, water parks, nightlife areas, and transportation center.

Special Features: Boat access to the Magic Kingdom makes getting to the fun a trip in itself.

The Wilderness Lodge is one of our favorites for the atmosphere, so if the price and accommodations are right, this could be a great choice. Studios and Villas cost much as at other resorts in this category, but certainly the outdoor and lakeside activities in the area make it the best alternative if you want to experience more than just the theme parks. This is a top choice for groups with kids. This is one of the Disney Vacation Club resorts.

ALERT TO ALL MILITARY!

Are you in the Army, Navy, Air Force, or Marines? Well, Disney has a hotel just for you! Shades of Green is a Disney-run hotel exclusively reserved for military personnel and their families. Make sure you consider this option if you are coming to Walt Disney World

Website: www.shadesofgreen.org

Location: Magic Kingdom Area ㉒

Transportation: Bus to all theme parks, water parks, nightlife areas, and transportation center.

Special Features: AAFES General Store

Shades of Green is an Armed Forces Recreation Center (AFRC) available to eligible members of the U.S. Armed Forces community, Department of Defense civilians, and their families. Managed by Disney, it gives you all the same benefits as a traditional Disney Resort guest. Room rates are dependent upon military grade and type of room, but traditionally range from $76.00 to $116.00. Check out their website for more information, or call their reservation desk from Monday through Friday from 0830 to 1700 hours (see, I know a little military-speak!) at (888) 593-2242.

A Disney Hotel Option: Hotel Plaza Boulevard

There are a number of hotels located on Disney property, and they offer another class of stay. Mostly located on Hotel Plaza Boulevard (in the Downtown Disney area), these seven hotels put you in the heart of Walt Disney World, though you are not getting all the same perks as if you were staying in a Disney-run resort. While they are technically "on-property," you should assume that they receive none of the traditional perks listed earlier in this chapter, though in a few cases they do have one or two of them. Ask them what they do offer, as some select packages do provide some, but not all, of these services.

Some of these non-Disney hotels have been around since the earliest years, when there was only the Magic Kingdom theme park, and they have traditionally offered some lower prices than the official resorts. Now that there are value resorts, some of the luster of these choices has worn off, but there are a few reasons why you should consider them:

caution These hotels use their own transportation to the Disney locations, and sometimes charge you a fee of around $5 per day for the service, so get all the facts before booking so you can budget correctly.

- Sometimes the deals here are really great.
- The rooms are comparable to the Moderate and even Deluxe resort rooms at Disney resorts.
- You can use existing points from hotel reward programs at Hilton, Marriott, Best Western, and Wyndham to book rooms.

 The best choices, due to comfort, location, and amenities, are the Hilton and the Wyndham Palace; for lower rates, try the Grovesnor.

- You can also earn points for a hotel reward program, something not available at traditional Disney resorts.

23 Doubletree Guest Suites in the Walt Disney World Resort

http://doubletree.hilton.com

2305 Hotel Plaza Boulevard

Lake Buena Vista, FL 32830

(407) 934-1000

Average price range: $125–139

This is a Hilton hotel chain, so if you have a frequent guest program there, you might be able to use points to stay, or you could earn points while there. Transportation is provided to all parks and Downtown Disney.

24 Best Western Lake Buena Vista Resort Hotel

www.bestwestern.com

2000 Hotel Plaza Boulevard

Lake Buena Vista, FL 32830

(407) 828-2424

Average price range: $109–169

There is a $5 daily resort fee that pays for transportation to all parks and Downtown Disney.

25 Hotel Royal Plaza in the Walt Disney World Resort

http://www.royalplaza.com/

1905 Hotel Plaza Blvd

PO Box 22203

Lake Buena Vista, FL 32830

(407) 828-2828

Average price range: $109–$169

Recently refurbished after suffering damage from the 2004 hurricane season, the hotel offers some updated styles and accommodations.

26 Courtyard Orlando Lake Buena Vista at Vista Centre

www.marriott.com

8501 Palm Parkway

Lake Buena Vista, FL 32836

(407) 239-6900

Average price range: $79–$149

Transportation provided to all four parks.

27 Grovesnor Resort in the Walt Disney World Resort

www.grosvenorresort.com

1850 Hotel Plaza Boulevard

Lake Buena Vista, Florida 32830

(800) 624-4109

Average price range: $90–$100

The Grovesnor is one of the original hotels in this area, and is well known for the Murder Mystery Dinner and the daily Disney Character Breakfasts at the Baskervilles Restaurant. Purchases in all four parks can be delivered to your room, a rare option for a non-Disney run hotel, and they run shuttles to all four parks. Don't let the fact that this hotel is not some big national chain scare you away from checking them out, especially if a super-low rate is needed for your budget.

28 Hilton in the Walt Disney World Resort

www.hilton.com

1751 Hotel Plaza Boulevard

Lake Buena Vista, FL 32830

(407) 827-4000

Average price range: $152–$209

Hilton offers shuttles, shared with guests from the Wyndham, to all parks. A Benihana is located on the property, along with other restaurants. The hotel is one of the nicer properties in the area, and it hosts frequent business meetings and conventions onsite, so it has a more formal environment than other locations. Downtown Disney is within a short walking distance.

29 Wyndham Palace Resort & Spa in the Walt Disney World Resort

www.wyndham.com

1900 Buena Vista Drive

P.O. Box 22206

Lake Buena Vista, FL 32830

(407) 827-2727

Average price range: $125–$149

Along with the Hilton, this is one of the nicest hotels in Hotel Plaza Boulevard. It has a spa, and shares shuttles with Hilton to all the Disney parks. Like the Hilton, it also is within reasonable walking distance to Downtown Disney.

To do list

- ☐ Learn about off-property hotels affiliated with Walt Disney World
- ☐ Review hotels in the Kissimmee area
- ☐ Review hotels in or near Lake Buena Vista
- ☐ Review hotels in the International Drive area

Off-Property Hotel Choices

In a recent online search for rooms in the Orlando area, more than 350 hotels came up. Needless to say, I can't review them all, and probably should not even try. There are a few things to share that can help you with planning if you are looking to stay off the Disney property, but still want to make sure you are getting the best deal possible.

You should know about the Walt Disney World Good Neighbor Hotel program. Hotels that carry this affiliation offer Disney packages that can include tickets, transportation, and other perks and programs. These deals change constantly, but usually offer decent savings on a package if you are getting tickets, so consider them. The hotels differ a great deal, so make sure you check their sites.

There are also other hotels in the area, but some are a bit sketchy. I would suggest that if you can't find something adequate after reviewing the onsite properties and the Good Neighbor hotels, you are going to find your selections limited, and your distance from the parks pretty significant. Good Neighbor Hotels are located in the areas of International Drive, Lake Buena Vista, and Celebration/Kissimmee.

tip Have you still not found the right hotel? Well, I have one other suggestion, and it is right in the neighborhood. The Gaylord Palms Resort is a great Florida-themed hotel with far better than average rooms and a great near-Disney location. It may not be a Disney hotel, or even an affiliated hotel, but it is one of my favorites. The big convention space can mean that the hotel is fully booked at certain times, so plan ahead. I have never been disappointed, and the rooms, as well as the Canyon Ranch Spa, can make an otherwise hectic vacation seem a bit luxurious. Check it out at www. gaylordhotels.com/gaylordpalms or call them at 407.586.0000.

Things You'll Need

- Computer
- Internet access

Kissimmee Area

This is the best location for getting to the parks as quickly as possible, especially Animal Kingdom and Magic Kingdom. Celebration Hotel is especially nice for a more upscale and relaxed experience, particularly if you have an all-adult group. Here are some of the best hotels in this area:

- Celebration Hotel (www.celebrationhotel.com, 407-566-1844)
- Clarion Hotel Maingate (www.choicehotels.com, 407-396-4000)
- Doubletree Resorts Orlando—Villas at Maingate (www.hilton.com, 407-397-0555)

- Holiday Inn Maingate West (www.holiday-inn.com, 407-396-1100)
- Holiday Villas (www.holidayvillas.com, 1-800-344-3959)
- Homewood Suites by Hilton (www.hilton.com, 407-396-2229)
- La Quinta Inn Lakeside (www.laquinta.com, 407-396-2222)
- Quality Suites Maingate East (www.choicehotels.com, 407-396-8040)
- Ramada Plaza Hotel & Inn Gateway (www.ramada.com, 407-846-2713)

Lake Buena Vista

This area is great for getting to Downtown Disney, though traffic is pretty thick and the strip malls are pretty annoying and unsightly. The Caribe Royale has not gotten the best marks, but the Sheraton Vistana Resort has more than a few fans among those looking for larger accommodations. The SunSpree has a frenetic, kid-crazy feel, but it might be ideal for a family with lots of kids to distract. Here are some of the best hotels in this area:

- Buena Vista Suites (www.buenavistasuites.com, 1-800-537-7737)
- Caribe Royale All Suite Resort and Convention Center (www.cariberoyale.com, 1-800-823-8300)
- Courtyard by Marriott Lake Buena Vista at Vista Center (www.marriott.com, 407-239-6900)
- Doubletree Club Hotel Lake Buena Vista (www.hilton.com, 407-239-4646)
- Embassy Suites Hotel Lake Buena Vista Resort (www.hilton.com, 407-239-1144)
- Fairfield Inn Orlando Lake Buena Vista in The Marriott Village (www.marriott.com, 407-938-9001)
- Holiday Inn SunSpree Resort (www.holiday-inn.com, 407-239-4500)
- Radisson Inn Lake Buena Vista (www.radisson.com, 407-239-8400)
- Sheraton Safari Hotel Lake Buena Vista (www.starwood.com, 407-239-0444)
- Sheraton Vistana Resort (www.starwood.com, 407-239-3100)

International Drive

Hotels in this area are ideal if you are going to visit Universal Studios or other theme parks. The traffic is very heavy, and it will cause longer commute times to Disney, but you also get a lot of dining options here, as there are numerous chain restaurants in the area. The Peabody is great for a more upscale experience, complete with ducks in the lobby fountain! I recommend dinner at *Café Tu Tu Tango* for a tapas-style meal that is great for large groups looking to have a good time! Here are some of the hotels in the area:

- Doubletree Castle Hotel (www.hilton.com, 407-345-1511)
- Embassy Suites Hotel Orlando International Drive South (www.hilton.com, 407-352-1400)
- Hampton Inn Convention Center (www.hilton.com, 407-354-4447)
- La Quinta Inn International Drive (www.laquinta.com, 407-351-1660)
- The Peabody Orlando (www.peabodyorlando.com, 407-352-4000)

Summary

So by now you have figured out where you are going to stay, but what are you going to eat? You can't very well come back to the hotel for every meal, and with so many food choices throughout Walt Disney World, why would you want to? So tuck in your napkin, lick your lips, and get ready to choose from some of the most fun, entertaining, and delicious restaurants you will ever see!

Dining at WDW: The Real Magic of Disney World

3

In this chapter:

* Find out about restaurants all around the World (*Walt Disney* World that is!)
* Figure out what choices are the best for your taste and budget
* Learn how to meet your favorite Disney characters at meals

If your idea of theme park food variety is having cheese added to your hamburger, you are in for a big surprise. Walt Disney World has grown over the years to include an amazing array of dining selections. There are counter service fast food joints, elegant fine dining, and food stands with everything from soft drinks and ice cream to fresh fruit and roasted turkey legs. You can select cuisines from all around the world, or some really great American classics. You may also be surprised by a growing effort to bring healthier choices to the parks and to meet specialty diet requirements.

Making your dining arrangements ahead of time is very important. Since the right meals can make a vacation, underestimating your true food costs could just as easily ruin it. So why is planning important? Well, some restaurants are so popular that you have to make an advance reservation weeks before you arrive if you want to get in. You also want to be sure to budget out what you are going to spend on food. While there are dining options to fit all cost ranges, it would be easy to overspend if you don't pay attention.

So what you should do with this chapter is get an idea of where you want to eat, what it will cost

For Advanced Reservations, call 407-WDW-DINE or 407-939-3463

you, and for which meals you will need to make an advance reservation arrangement ahead of time.

In this chapter, the restaurants are organized by location, and then by type. At most places throughout Walt Disney World you have the option of dining at a Table Service restaurant, a Counter Service restaurant, or to simply pick up a snack along the way, so I have organized them in those categories. So pick your favorites, plan your dining, and *bon appétit!*

To do list

- ☐ Review the dining options based on where you plan on being for each meal during your vacation
- ☐ Select the restaurant that best suits your group's appetite and budget
- ☐ Schedule the advanced reservation arrangements for all your meals

Scheduling Meals: The Disney Advanced Reservations System

Walt Disney World restaurants now accept reservations, but they are a bit different than what you might be used to. The system is easy. Simply call 704-WDW-DINE, which translates to 704-939-3463. Tell them what restaurant you would like to go to, party size, desired time, and so on. Your advanced reservation schedule means that when you arrive and check in, you are placed ahead of anyone who is waiting for a table but doesn't have an advanced reservation arrangement. And since they only accept a limited number of advanced reservations per hour, it is in most respects exactly like a reservation. You can write down your confirmation number on the Trip Card in the back of the book, and you should plan to arrive at the restaurant 10–15 minutes before your seating time. You can make an advanced reservation arrangement for most Disney restaurant as early as 90 days ahead of time.

note In all my travels to Walt Disney World I have never been seated more than 10 minutes after my scheduled advanced reservations time. I am sure someone out there has a story of disappointment, but for me it has worked as well, or better, than most reservation systems at restaurants back home.

If you know of a few restaurants where you really want to dine, make those advanced registration calls from home before you leave on your trip. In the cases of these more sought-after restaurants, you will want to call in exactly 90 days ahead of time, and as soon as the phone lines open at 7 a.m. Eastern time:

- *Once Upon a Time Breakfast* at *Cinderella's Royal Table*
- Lunch at the *Crystal Palace*
- Dinners on certain holidays (New Year's, Christmas, Thanksgiving)
- Dinners at restaurants with a view of fireworks
- The *Disney Spirit of Aloha* show at the Polynesian Resort
- The Hoop de Doo Musical Review

note Advanced reservations, which used to be known as "Priority Seating," are basically like reservations, but with a few differences. But there is one restaurant that does take standard reservations. *Victoria & Albert's*, which is located at the Grand Floridian Resort, accepts them. It is the most upscale restaurant in all of Walt Disney World, and the experience is expensive but exceptional.

Also, the dinner shows require advanced reservations. The Spirit of Aloha and Hoop-Dee-Doo Musical Review dinner shows allow for reservations to be made up to two years in advance, and the Mickey's Backyard BBQ can be booked one year in advance.

Making the Most of Character Meals

Whether you are eating at a buffet-style restaurant or one where you order from the menu, the character meals follow the same basic pattern. A set list of characters makes the rounds to each table, stopping for photos and to sign autographs. The characters circulate frequently and are meticulous about hitting each table, so you don't have to worry about being overlooked.

Character meals can be the single best experience for a child on a Disney vacation. There is something special about Mickey Mouse coming to visit you at your dinner table, as opposed to waiting in line for hours to meet him in a park.

I recommend that if you have kids, you get at least one character meal during your stay. I also think that you can overdo them. Don't make every dinner a character meal; set aside some meals for discussing the day's events. It will make you enjoy the vacation even more!

UNDERSTANDING THE RESTAURANT LISTINGS

The restaurant listings include several basic codes for you to identify what is the right place for you. So what do these symbols mean? Some reflect cost per person; others tell you what meals they offer, and if they are character meals. Here is a quick key:

$ $0–10 per person

$$ $10–20 per person

$$$ $20–30 per person

$$$$ More than $30 per person

☼ Open for Breakfast

☼ Open for Lunch

☾ Open for Dinner

♀ Great for snacks

B Open for a Character Meal Breakfast

L Open for a Character Meal Lunch

D Open for a Character Meal Dinner

Finally, the listing tells you what food type the restaurant serves, and then there is a brief description of what the atmosphere and food are like.

Things You'll Need

- ❑ Your Trip Card
- ❑ Pen or pencil and paper

Dining at the Magic Kingdom

While Walt Disney World's single most popular meal reservation is located within the Magic Kingdom, many find that in general the restaurant selection here is pretty

For Advanced Reservations, call 407-WDW-DINE or 407-939-3463

limited, with little variety, as compared to other parks at WDW. But that is not to say that the food is not good. The choices for lunch are certainly going to fulfill most groups' needs, just with less flair and selection than in other parks. As for dinner, you still have several solid restaurant choices, but remember that there is no alcohol in the Magic Kingdom, so that may make you want to swing dinner plans somewhere else.

> **note** **The Best Dining at the Magic Kingdom**
>
> **Best Overall Dining:** *Once Upon a Time Breakfast* at *Cinderella's Royal Table*
>
> **Best Table Service Restaurant:** *The Crystal Palace*
>
> **Best Quick Service:** *Pecos Bill Café*
>
> **Best Snacks:** *Aloha Isle*

Table Service

Cinderella's Royal Table
$$$ ☙B ☙L ☾ American

The *Once Upon a Time Breakfast*, located inside Cinderella's Castle, is the single most popular meal throughout Walt Disney World. Trust me when I say that the Advanced Reservations phones light up at 7 a.m. months ahead of time to book seats at this character meal. So is it worth it? If you have a little princess in your group (or prince, for that matter), it is. Although the menu is standard, the setting inside the castle is magical, even for adults. Lunch has recently been changed to a character meal as well, so check on times then if the breakfast if booked up.

The Crystal Palace
$$ ☙B ☙L ☙D American Buffet

The wait here can be long, especially for lunch. The food is traditional, and well prepared, so if that is the kind of meal experience you are looking for, go for it. This is another place where advanced reservations are a must, and probably one you want to make before you leave on your vacation. Winnie the Pooh and friends are the constant character hosts at this restaurant.

Liberty Tree Tavern
$$$ ☼ ☙D American

The Liberty Tree Tavern sports traditional American fare in a Revolutionary-era setting, smack dab in the middle of Liberty Square. I recommend the poultry selections or the carved meats. Don't come here for lunch if you are in a rush, as it can take some time.

For Advanced Reservations, call 407-WDW-DINE or 407-939-3463

The Plaza Restaurant

$$ ☼ ☾ American

Enjoy the casual charm of Main Street U.S.A. in this bright, open restaurant decorated with early 1900s décor. The table service is a bit quicker than usual, though the wait for a table can be significant. Stick to the sandwiches here, and let the soda fountain tempt you with something sweet at meal's end.

Tony's Town Square

$$ ☼ ☾ Italian

This Main Street U.S.A. restaurant inspired by the movie *Lady and the Tramp* offers prompt table-service. I recommend sticking with the more traditional pasta dishes.

Counter Service

Aloha Island—Pineapple based snacks including the famous Dole Whip

Casey's Corner—The best hot dog in all of WDW

Columbia Harbour House—Burgers, as well as soups and salads

Cosmic Ray's Starlight Café—Traditional burgers and chicken choices

Main Street Bakery—An incredible array of sweets

Pecos Bill Café—The #1 burger stand in the Kingdom. Why? The fixings bar!

The Pinocchio Village Haus—Burgers, fries, and dogs

El Pirata y El Perico Restaurant—Fast food of a Mexican variety

The Tomorrowland Terrace Noodle Station—Salads and noodle dishes

MUST-DO MEALS AT WDW

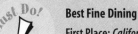

These are our favorite dining experience at Walt Disney World.

Best Fine Dining

First Place: *California Grill* at the *Contemporary Resort*

Second Place: *Victoria & Albert's* at the *Grand Floridian Resort*

Best Table Service Casual Dining

First Place: *50's Prime Time Café* at Disney-MGM

Second Place: *Wolfgang Puck's Café* at Downtown Disney

Best Character Meals

First Place: *Once Upon a Time Breakfast* at *Cinderella's Royal Table* at the Magic Kingdom

Second Place: *Breakfastosaurus* at *Restaurantosaurus* at the Animal Kingdom

For Advanced Reservations, call 407-WDW-DINE or 407-939-3463

Best Entertainment Dining (Non-Character)

First Place: *Hoop-Dee-Doo Musical Review* at *Fort Wilderness Resort and Campground*

Second Place: *Disney Spirit of Aloha Show* at the *Polynesian Resort*

Honorary Mention: *Whispering Canyon Café* at the *Wilderness Lodge*

Best Quick Service Meals

First Place: *Flame Tree Barbecue* at Animal Kingdom

Second Place: *Sunset Ranch Market* at Disney MGM

Best Treats

First Place: Candy Apples at *Starring Rolls Café* in Disney-MGM

Second Place: Fudge and other sweets on the BoardWalk

Honorable Mention: Turkey legs on Sunset Boulevard in Disney MGM

Dining at Epcot

Food is a major attraction at Epcot, at least in the World Showcase. Make absolutely certain that when you visit this park, you schedule at least one meal here, as you will find the selection and quality pretty impressive. Also consider dining in a less traditional way, by simply sampling snack-sized bites from the open-air stands at several different counties (see "Snackapalooza" in Chapter 5, "Epcot: Bringing the World and the Future Together"). It gives you a chance to experience some new flavors, and could be less time-consuming and less expensive than a sit-down dinner at one of the national pavilions.

note Here are Epcot's "best":

Best Fine Dining: A tie between *Marrakesh*, *Akershus*, and the *Biergarten*, for the flavors of countries that you may not find at home with this level of atmosphere.

Best Quick Service: *Sunshine Season Food Fair*.

Honorable Mention: Dining outside at *The Rose & Crown* for the view of the Illuminations fireworks show.

Table Service

Restaurant Akershus

$$$ B L D **Norwegian/Scandinavian**

When was the last time you said to your family, "Hey, let's go eat Norwegian!"? Well, after eating here, you probably will. The character meals here are great, with a setting worthy of a princess in the castle-like interior, and hosted by many Disney movie heroines. The selection of cheeses, meats, and other smoked foods make for an experience and fulfilling meal, though it may not be what younger, finicky customers were expecting.

Biergarten Restaurant
$$$ ☼ ☾ German

Buffet style dining with a live band makes for an Oktoberfest-style good time. This is great for families, and especially fun for an all-adult group looking to kick it up a notch. Try the fine selection of meats and classic German dishes for your best experience.

Bistro de Paris
$$$$ ☾ French

This *prix-fixe* menu (one standard price for the meal, and you select from among three to four items for each course) is an elegant experience and a culinary masterpiece. With a second floor view of the firework and light shows, this could be a wonderful romantic experience, if you can afford it.

Le Cellier Steakhouse
$$$ ☼ ☾ Steakhouse

Located in the *Canada Pavilion*, the wine-cellar atmosphere and excellent steak selections here make for a romantic setting. Not a great place for kids and a bit heavy for lunch, this restaurant offers a slightly less upscale (and less expensive) experience than *Shula's* in the nearby *Dolphin Hotel*.

Les Chefs de France
$$$$ ☼ ☾ French

This restaurant is only a bit less expensive than the *Bistro de Paris*, but it reminds many of a classic Parisian café setting, complete with the fun of watching the people walking by outside. French classics here include the haute cuisine dishes you might expect, along with popular street choices such as Croque Monsieur (a ham and cheese sandwich, Parisian style) that are ideal for kids hesitant to trying new things. This is a great dinner selection for groups with kids who want to swing a bit more upscale.

Coral Reef Restaurant
$$$$ ☼ ☾ Seafood

You get top-notch seafood here, as well as a great show, courtesy of the gigantic aquarium that is the *Living Seas Pavilion*. Divers will occasionally swim by to entertain, as do sharks, grouper, rays, and other amazing tropical fish. The seafood is excellent, but the upscale and elegant setting may not be ideal for groups with smaller children, who can only be fascinated by the fish swimming by for so long.

The Garden Grill Restaurant
$$$ ☙L ☙D American

Located in the *Land Pavilion*, much of the food here is raised in the pavilion through hydroponics and other advanced agriculture technologies. Characters come around to the tables, and the food is country/American, featuring seafood, steaks, and some great produce.

Restaurant Marrakesh
$$$ ☼ ☾ Moroccan

You will feel like you are in Casablanca as belly dancers entertain in this intricately detailed restaurant. The lamb is excellent, and if you want to get a real feel for North African cuisine, make sure you opt for whatever sampler options they have on the menu. Ask for a table either close to the entertainment in the middle of the room or up on the highest tier in the back of the room, which also provides a great view. This is another great place to bring kids when you are looking for a somewhat upscale experience.

Nine Dragons Restaurant
$$ ☼ ☾ Chinese

The Chinese cuisine here tastes a great deal more authentic than the average delivery service back home, so consider it if you like Chinese and want to see what it is like when made right.

L'Originale Alfredo di Roma Ristorante
$$$$ ☼ ☾ Italian

Traditional but authentic Italian fare is hidden away in this less-traveled restaurant located in the back of the *Italy Pavilion*. Try the Fettuccini Alfredo, or one of the other specialties of the house.

Rose & Crown Dining Room
$$ ☼ ☾ English/Pub

This and *Nine Dragons* are the two table-service restaurants in the World Showcase that are easiest on your wallet. The food here is down to earth, featuring fish and chips and other traditional pub food.

San Angel Inn
$$ ☼ ☾ Mexican

Seated in a courtyard inside the Mexico Pavilion pyramid, with a view of a volcano and a village market, you can sample authentic Mexican food created by a famed Mexico City restaurateur. There is no artificial nacho cheese here, only classic molé sauces and a selection of seafood, beef, and pork-based entrées that are a true treat!

Teppanyaki Dining Room
$$$ ☼ ☾ Japanese

Gather 'round a grill that serves as your table and be amazed as the knives and food fly around the room. There is nothing new here if you have been to a Benihana's back home, but it is a great social meal, and a great place to talk about the day's events.

Tempura Kiku
$$ ☼ ☾ Japanese

Belly up to the sushi bar and satisfy that yen, complete with many traditional rolls and nigiri, as well as a few you may not have heard of before.

tip The Rose & Crown is one of the most popular restaurants at Epcot, because the patio seats offer the best views of the Illuminations fireworks show. Make a priority seating for a late dinner, and then arrive well before your time and let them know you want to sit outside to see the show after dinner. They will do their best to help you, but no promises.

Counter Service

World Showcase

Boulangerie Patisserie—Classic French pastries

La Cantina De San Angel—Tex-mex snacks, but a great afternoon break

Harry Ramsden—Fish and chips as good as you get in the *Rose & Crown*

Kringla Bakeri Og Kafe—Norwegian pastries

Liberty Inn—Burgers, chicken, and the other standards. Great for kids who don't want to try new things.

For Advanced Reservations, call 407-WDW-DINE or 407-939-3463

Lotus Blossom Café—Egg rolls and some other take out standards

Sommerfest—Beer, pretzels, and sausages

Tangierine Café—The best counter service in Epcot; try the lamb shawarma

Yakitori House—Sushi, noodle bowls, and other Japanese treats

Futureworld

Electric Umbrella Restaurant—Another standard fast-food restaurant

Sunshine Season Food Fair—Food court with great variety and indoor seating

Dining at Disney-MGM

Disney-MGM ranks second behind Epcot as the best overall park to dine in. Make sure you are here for a lunch. Interestingly enough, there are no character meals of note within this park, but there are plenty of character meeting areas in the park, so you should be fine.

note Here's the Best Dining at Disney-MGM:

Best Overall Dining: *50's Prime Time Diner*

Best Full Service Restaurant: *The Brown Derby*

Best Quick Service: *Sunset Ranch Market*

Best Snacks: Turkey legs on Sunset Boulevard

Honorable Mention: *The Sci-Fi Dine-In Theater*

Table Service

50's Prime Time Café
$$ ☼ ☾ **American**

Comfort food with a side of attitude. This is our favorite "experience" meal, where you dine at the kitchenette table in your mom's house. That is, if your mom was stuck back in the 50s. Meatloaf, roasted chicken, and other American classics are served by a staff that will make you eat your green beans, keep your elbows off the table, and say "please" and "thank you." This is truly fun for all ages, so make an advanced reservation for a lunch here, and order a shake as you leave.

The Hollywood Brown Derby
$$$$ ☼ ☾ **American**

Modeled after the famed (and long-since closed) Hollywood star hangout, the menu has some selection, but the Cobb Salad is the star, as are the authentic rolls. Perhaps not the intimate setting you might expect for the cost of the meal, however.

For Advanced Reservations, call 407-WDW-DINE or 407-939-3463

Hollywood & Vine
$$ ☾ American/Buffet

Open only for dinner, the broad spread of choices is especially good for large groups who may have a problem coming to a common decision on what they want to eat. The 50s soda shop interior is bright and cheerful, and makes for a fun group setting.

Mama Melrose's Ristorante Italiano
$$ ☼ ☾ Italian

Try the pizzas, or one of the other Italian classics, in this friendly and cheerful locale that provides a nice alternative to the higher price or heavily themed alternatives. If you are in a hurry, load up on one of their pastas.

note If you plan on going to the Fantasmic! show at Disney-MGM, why not try a "Fantasmic! Dining Experience"? This special package combines an advanced reservation at select table service restaurants in Disney-MGM along with a VIP ticket for the Fantasmic! show, at no extra charge. Since lines for the nighttime show can be long, this guarantees you a seat at the show, gets you to the front of the line, and lets you enjoy a nice meal.

Sci-Fi Dine-In Theater
$$ ☼ ☾ American

Your table is a car at a drive-in, watching 50s-era sci-fi movie clips. This is a popular family choice with carhop waiters bringing you burgers and sandwiches that typically are a bit better than those at the counter-service restaurants. Order a shake to go before you leave; they are great, and serve as an excellent portable dessert.

Counter Service

ABC Commissary—Burgers, as well as Cuban sandwiches and other specialties from Asia and South America

Backlot Express—Standard burger and fries offerings

Dinosaur Gertie's Ice Cream of Extinction—Ice cream treats

Sunset Ranch Market—The best counter-service restaurant at Disney-MGM with outdoor dining and a wide selection, including turkey legs

Starring Rolls Café—Candy apples, pastries, fudge, and other goodies

Toy Story Pizza Planet Arcade—Pizzas and salads

For Advanced Reservations, call 407-WDW-DINE or 407-939-3463

Dining at the Animal Kingdom

Dining choices are pretty few and far between here, but they still manage to surprise you with some great finds. One of the best character meals, one of the best counter-service experiences, all this and more reside right here in the newest of the parks.

> **note** Here are the best bets for dining at Animal Kingdom:
>
> **Best Full Service Restaurant:** *Breakfastosaurus* at *Restaurantosaurus*
>
> **Best Quick Service:** *Flame Tree Barbecue*
>
> **Best Snacks:** Fresh Fruit at *Harambe Fruit Market*

Table Service

Rainforest Café—Animal Kingdom

$$$ ☌ ☼ ☾ **American**

This national chain has two restaurants at Walt Disney World (the other is in Downtown Disney). The selection is broad, with pastas, sandwiches, and more substantial entrées as well. Entry from both inside and outside the park entrance is available.

Counter Service

Chakranadi Chicken Shop—Stir fry and easy to carry Asian specialties

Flame Tree Barbeque—Excellent BBQ with exotic, secluded seating areas

Harambe Fruit Market—A great selection of fresh fruits

Kusafiri Coffee Shop—Pastries and coffee

Pizzafari—Fast food, Italian style

Restaurantosaurus—Traditional burger counter that transforms to a character buffet for breakfast

Tusker House Restaurant—Offers burgers and great vegetarian selections

> **note** For lunch and dinner, *Restaurantosaurus* is just another burger counter restaurant, but for breakfast you are dropped into a campground dining experience with many of your favorite characters at what is known as *Breakfastosaurus*. This is definitely an Advanced Reservation must, where campfire stoves serve as chafing dishes for the breakfast buffet, and Donald Duck makes sure that your table is happy with the grub.

Dining at the BoardWalk

The BoardWalk is a great place to spend an evening. There are entertainers, sights, sounds, activities, and some food choices to make the night complete. These restaurants also serve as the restaurants for the *BoardWalk Inn* and *Villas*.

> **note** Here are the best dining spots at the BoardWalk:
>
> **Best Full Service Restaurant:** *Flying Fish Café*
>
> **Best Quick Service:** Spoodles window-service pizza
>
> **Best Snacks:** *Seashore Sweets*

Table Service

Big River Grille & Brewing Works
$$ ☼ ☾ **American**

Grab an outdoor table if the weather is right, and get a free show with your meal. The people-watching is fun, and the food is a great mix of lighter sandwich and salad entrées. More than just pub food, *Big River* has a good selection, and the beers are great too!

ESPN Club
$$ ☼ ☾ **American**

Sports bar food has found some life here, where the traditional fare is done well. Sandwiches, burgers, and a selection of alternatives make this a great place to take in a game, celebrate with friends, or just catch a quick dinner. You won't rave about the food, but you won't be disappointed either.

Flying Fish Café
$$$$ ☾ **Seafood**

This elegant and expensive seafood restaurant is a worthwhile indulgence. The service is great, the food is delicious, and the ambience is very cool in an eclectic way. If you are a seafood fan, this is your best choice in all of Walt Disney World.

Spoodles
$$$ ⚞ ☾ **American/Mediterranean**

The breakfast is standard American fare, with no surprises. The service is fairly efficient, as they know you have a theme park day on your mind. Dinner is when things turn Mediterranean, with cuisines from around the sea, but primarily Italian selections. Priority Seating is a must for dinner, as it is the most family-friendly choice in the area.

For Advanced Reservations, call 407-WDW-DINE or 407-939-3463

Counter Service

Seashore Sweets—Ice cream, sweets, and baked goods.

BoardWalk Bakery—Coffee, bagels, pastries, and an egg and ham burrito to die for!

Spoodles Window Service—Great pizza!

Dining at Downtown Disney

Downtown Disney is split into three areas, and for the most part the dining is found at either end, with few dining choices found in Pleasure Island in the middle.

Table Service

Bongos Cuban Café
$$$ ☼ ☾ **Cuban**

Owned by Gloria and Emilio Estefan, the food at this cool, chic café is Cuban inspired, with several other options based on popular Latin American and Caribbean recipes. This is a great choice as your starting point for a special night out on the town. The café welcomes families, but seems more like an adult's dining choice.

Cap'n Jack's Restaurant
$$ ☼ ☾ **American**

Cap'n Jack's is primarily a seafood restaurant, but it has an extensive non-fish menu as well. It really tries to be an all-pleasing casual dining locale, and it is successful as a non-threatening place for families and adult-only groups at the same time. Try the chowder or any of the seafood choices.

Fulton's Crab House
$$$$ ☼ ☾ **Seafood**

Located between the Marketplace and Pleasure Island, diners here eat crab and other seafood on a permanently docked riverboat. The crab is good, and this is a

> **note** The BoardWalk is also lined with several stands that serve sweets, beverages, and other tasty temptations, so look for a carnival or state fair favorite along the wooden walk. Most are not open until the evening, so regardless of where you had dinner, you should let this be your dessert destination.

> **note** Downtown Disney's best dining spots:
>
> **Best Full Service Restaurant:** *Wolfgang Puck's Café*
>
> **Best Quick Service:** *Earl of Sandwich Restaurant*
>
> **Best Snacks:** *Ghirardelli Soda Fountain & Chocolate Shop*

popular place, though expensive for cafeteria-style seating. You might be able to get a more elegant experience elsewhere for the money, though the crab probably won't be this good.

House of Blues
$$$☀ ☼ ☾ Creole/Cajun

The restaurant is basically just open for lunch and dinner, but the Sunday Gospel Brunch that the chain has become famous for combines a unique blend of dining and entertainment that you will find nowhere else in Walt Disney World. Lunch and dinner menus tend toward spicier foods, and the atmosphere is one that teens and adult will particularly enjoy, though guests of all ages are welcome.

Planet Hollywood
$$$ ☼ ☾ American

Planet Hollywood seems to be more about the experience than the food. While the memorabilia on the walls is interesting, the wait to get in and the tab at the end of the meal make this chain restaurant one that might be avoided. Food is pretty standard chain fare, combining high-end burgers, sandwiches, pasta, and other entrées.

Portobello Yacht Club
$$$$ ☼ ☾ Italian

The food is excellent, and the lakeside views make for a pleasant experience as you select from wood-oven-baked pizzas, pastas, and other Mediterranean selections. The food is great, though your bill will grow quickly if you don't watch yourself. Located next to *Fulton's Crab House*, between *Pleasure Island* and the *Marketplace*, this is one of the nicer, if somewhat expensive, dining options in Downtown Disney.

Rainforest Café
$$$ ☼ ☾ American

The second of two Rainforest Café's at Disney World (the other is at the Animal Kingdom Park), this is a great choice for lunch or dinner with kids. The atmosphere is vivid and captivating, and will keep kids busy for as long as you will be there. The food is good, too, with a wide selection of options, ranging from salads, to sandwiches, to other entrées.

Wolfgang Puck Café

$$$ ☼ ☾ **American**

The middle of the three Wolfgang Puck options (there is a quick-service *Wolfgang Puck Express* outside and a high end restaurant upstairs), this is an excellent option for diners at Downtown Disney. The prices are varied but reasonable, the selection is broad, and you get some world-class cuisine for standard chain prices. The atmosphere is fun but not comical, and is equally attractive for romantic dinners and family outings. The high-end restaurant upstairs is expensive, and probably one to go after only if you have a company expense account handy to absorb the pain.

Counter Service

Earl of Sandwich Restaurant—Fresh-made sandwiches for a quick lunch

Ghirardelli Soda Fountain & Chocolate Shop—Shakes and ice cream

McDonald's—The comfortable familiarity of something from home

Missing Link Sausage Company—Hot dog stand with great Philly cheese steak sandwiches

Wetzel's Pretzels—Pretzels and the basics of a burger/hot dog stand

Wolfgang Puck Express—Eclectic, fast lunch choices at two locations

Dining at the Resorts

Although you'll appreciate the good restaurants in the parks during the middle of the day, you need some good food at night, too, and probably a bit closer to your hotel room. Listed here are some of the best dining options throughout the resorts, either because of the food, the price, the convenience, or the experience.

note Disney transportation makes visiting any of the resort restaurants an easy proposition from your hotel, no matter where in Walt Disney World you're staying. All restaurants listed are table service, unless otherwise noted.

Deluxe Resorts

Most of the deluxe resorts also have counter-service restaurants that offer a consistent selection of burgers, pizza, and sandwiches. When you check in, the resort map will point these out. The deluxe resorts also offer some interesting table service dining options as well.

Disney's Animal Kingdom Lodge

Boma—Flavors of Africa
$$$ ☆ ☽ American/African

Breakfast is standard American fare, intended to power you up for a day at the parks. But at dinnertime they take the best of the African continent and serve it up buffet style so that you can experiment with several different flavors. This is a great place to get kids to try new things, since the food isn't too exotic.

Jiko—The Cooking Place
$$$$ ☽ African

Taste the flavors of Africa, tempered to meet North American tastes via a blend of Indian and Mediterranean influences. You may hate the word "fusion" when referred to cooking, but they have really fused the flavors together well for a unique and tasty experience at this more formal of the hotel's two African restaurants.

Disney's Beach Club Resort and Villas

Cape May Café
$$$ ☙B ☽ American

Breakfast is a character meal, served buffet style, with all the standard American offerings. The characters don't appear at dinner, but the buffet offers a variety of seafood options, as well as a good selection of meats and other goodies.

note The BoardWalk Inn and Villas do not offer any real dining options, since the BoardWalk is right outside with a great array of choices. See these restaurants in the *Dining at the BoardWalk* section in this chapter.

Disney's Contemporary Resort

California Grill
$$$$ ☽ American

This is, hands-down, my favorite restaurant in all of Walt Disney World. The food is exceptional, the service is some of the best I have ever experienced anywhere, and the views are breathtaking. Yes, it is expensive, and they do require resort casual attire (no bathing suits or t-shirts), but that is part of what makes it nice. You sit in the penthouse floor of the hotel with a bird's-eye view of the Magic Kingdom, and can watch it come to life (and light) in the evening. Time it so that you finish dinner just before the fireworks show from the Magic Kingdom, which you can take in with an after-dinner drink on the outdoor deck. Try the pork with polenta, and the sushi that is served with real wasabi. If you are on a romantic getaway and don't come here, shame on you!

Chef Mickey's
$$$ 🍂B 🍂D American

Always a full-blown character experience, Chef Mickey brings better-than-average buffet food into a chaotic but fun environment. There are so many Disney characters that you almost don't notice the monorail whizzing by overhead. The selection is very kid friendly, but adults can find something special, too. If you are not up for the character experience, don't even think of coming here.

Concourse Steakhouse
$$$ ☌ ☼ ☾ American/Steakhouse

A more casual steakhouse than most, this open-roofed restaurant looks up at the hotel's vast atrium, monorail and all. The breakfast is traditional American fare, while lunch and dinner change to a steakhouse menu. The prices are more reasonable than most upscale steakhouses, but the noisy interior, and the fact that guests can look down on you while you eat makes it a less than elegant experience.

Disney's Grand Floridian Resort & Spa

1900 Park Fare
$$$ 🍂B 🍂D American

Breakfast is with Mary Poppins and friends, while dinner is with Cinderella and her entourage. These buffet meals are on the pricier side, but the characters, particularly at dinner, are focused on what many little girls dream of when they come to Walt Disney World. There is also an afternoon tea with the characters from Alice in Wonderland. Check with the hotel for details.

Citricos
$$$$ ☾ Mediterranean

Citricos is an elegant locale with great food that is perfect for a special evening. The food is Spanish and Italian inspired, and brings a pleasant and relaxing conclusion to a hectic day at the parks.

For Advanced Reservations, call 407-WDW-DINE or 407-939-3463

Grand Floridian Café
$$☾ ☀ ☾ **American**

A casual lunch and dinner place, especially for families and those looking for a faster meal, but tired of grabbing burgers in the park. The lunch offerings lean toward salads and sandwiches, while dinner offers more elaborate entrées.

Narcoossee's
$$$$☾ **Seafood**

This pavilion offers a superb array of seafood, and a view of the lagoon that is hard to beat. The environment is decidedly less formal than the rest of this resort hotel, but it is still quite elegant and provides a romantic backdrop to the fantastic fare.

Victoria and Albert's
$$$$☾ **American**

Expect a tab upward of $100 each at the most elegant and high-end restaurant in all of Walt Disney World. The chefs here are extremely accommodating to special dietary needs and special occasions. Just let them know the particulars before you get there, and they will make you a meal that you will never forget. The prix-fixe meal (one standard price for the meal, and your choice from three or four sections for each course) changes daily and is customized to your party, including a personalized menu. A jacket is required for gentlemen, with appropriate similar attire for women as well. I know plenty of people who would never consider coming to Walt Disney World without eating here.

> **note** A great way to keep your meal spending down is to hit some of your favorite restaurants for lunch instead of dinner. Often, the same entrées cost less at lunch.

Disney's Polynesian Resort

Kona Café
$$$☾ ☀ ☾ **American**

There are some Asian-inspired foods here, with favorites like the Tonga Toast (banana stuffed toast), but the selection is pretty American in its approach. The décor is a bit more upscale and elegant than the rest of the resort, so it can be a nice change.

'Ohana
$$$ ᰂ B ☾ American

There is something fun about the locale that makes this a great place for a character breakfast, even though only the characters from *Lilo and Stitch* really fit with the décor. The food is basic American, served family style. The dinner is good, too, even though there are no characters. Skewered meats (kabobs) give you a lot of choices and new experiences.

Disney's Spirit of Aloha Show
$$$$ ☾ Polynesian

This replaced the old luau that was a long-standing popular experience at Walt Disney World. The show is better and the food is, too. This is an especially fun event for kids, as they can be part of the show. And the music, dancing, and other performances are truly spectacular. Since the meals are all-you-can-eat, you might plan for it to be a big end to a day where you did not have time for a large lunch. Priority Seating is a requirement, as they basically just have a few seatings per day.

Disney's Wilderness Lodge

Artist Point
$$$$ ☾ American

Dinner overlooking the rock formations, geysers, and babbling brook of the lodge's courtyard will make you forget that you are in Florida. The selection of fish and meats includes some more exotic options, such as bison. This is a nice place for a semi-formal, semi-casual dinner.

Whispering Canyon Café
$$$ ᰂ ☼ ☾ American

Tired of character meals, but want some fun for the kids? This is the place for you, where kids are part of the show, and the entertaining and energetic wait staff keeps you on your toes. The high-energy, family-style dining experience is not used as an excuse to cover up mediocre food. The barbecue is really great, and all the sides are good too. Just don't come here looking for a sedate and fancy time. This meal is highly recommended for families.

Disney's Yacht Club Resort

Yacht Club Galley
$$$ ☼ ☀ ☾ **American**

The galley offers à la carte dining for all meals, but also offers a standard breakfast buffet option as well. This is a good multi-purpose restaurant with a selection of soups, sandwiches, and other traditional American entrées.

Yachtsman Steakhouse
$$$$ ☾ **Steakhouse**

This is a casual steakhouse, offering an array of steaks, as well as seafood entrées.

Moderate Resorts

The moderate resorts all have food courts that offer a good selection of fast foods, usually including burgers, chicken, and pizza. These courts are somewhat festive and the food is good, so take advantage of them as a way to keep your budget in check, and to enjoy meals where you don't want to get dressed up and go out. Below are some table service selections that you can also find at these resorts.

Disney's Caribbean Beach Resort

Shutters at Old Port Royale
$$ ☀ ☾ **Caribbean**

Several Caribbean-inspired entrées join American favorites to make this an affordable and fun dining experience.

Disney's Coronado Springs Resort

Maya Grill
$$$ ☼ ☾ **American**

Don't let the name fool you; this is not a Mexican restaurant, though there are some Mexican entrées on the menu. The breakfast is a buffet; the dinner à la carte.

Disney's Port Orleans Resort

Boatwright's Dining Hall
$$☾☽ American

A great selection in a casual dining environment makes for a nice, relaxing environment to start or end a day. Southern breakfast specialties make breakfast more than just another à la carte experience.

Value Resorts

All of the Disney Value Resorts (All-Star Movie, Music, and Sports, and Pop Century) have cafeteria-style food courts that offer a great variety of food choices, changing throughout the day to match different hungers at different meal times. There is also a pizza stand that stays open late for carryout, and all offer in-room pizza delivery.

Other Resorts

Many of the other resorts in and around Walt Disney World have some interesting dining options. Here are just a few

Fort Wilderness Resort and Campground

The Hoop-Dee-Doo Musical Review
$$$$☽ American

This is one of the longtime favorite dinner shows at Walt Disney World, and it is one of the restaurants where an Advanced Reservation is a must. This show features a festive western theme that is perfect for the whole family. The food is basic American, featuring barbeque, chicken, and traditional sides.

Mickey's Backyard BBQ
$$$$☽D American

Technically not a character meal, you might get to see Mickey and Minnie at this covered outdoor dinner experience. Barbeque, chicken, and other picnic favorites are served under a covered seating area while an entertaining musical show keeps your toes tapping. This is only open from March to December, and can be cancelled if the weather gets nasty.

Trail's End Restaurant
$$ ☀ ☾ American

This buffet restaurant offers standard American fare, and is a great place for a larger group that has a million different tastes in mind.

Walt Disney World Dolphin

Shula's Steak House
$$$$ ☾ Steakhouse

This national chain of upscale steakhouses may be the best steak you can get in all of Walt Disney World. The price tag is high, but the posh atmosphere and excellent beef justify the expense.

Todd English's bluezoo
$$$$ ☾ Seafood

This is the most hip and modern club/restaurant at Walt Disney World, and a trendy haunt for some of the locals as well. Seafood selection is excellent, and the presentation and flavors match the suave interior. This is a great romantic getaway with a stylish flavor.

Walt Disney World Swan

Garden Grove Cafe
$$$ ☀ D American

Breakfast is a buffet, lunch is à la carte, and both bring a predictable spread of selections. At dinner time it is transformed into *Gulliver's Grill* for a character meal. This dinnertime buffet has not gotten very good marks as a character meal, and might not be your best bet for thrilling your kids.

Palio
$$$ ☾ Italian

This serene restaurant is perfectly matched to the quite ambience of its host hotel, the Swan. In addition to traditional southern Italian cuisine, Palio also offers select specials from other regions, all prepared with a modern and elegant twist.

For Advanced Reservations, call 407-WDW-DINE or 407-939-3463

Kimono's
$$☾ Sushi

The décor sets the mood with elegant black lacquer and colorful kimonos on the walls. The sushi is great, and the restaurant turns into a lively bar scene later in the evening, complete with karaoke.

Disney's Saratoga Springs Resort & Spa

The Artists Pallette (Counter Service)
$☼ ☼ ☾ American

Counter service and shopping to provide you the basics without having to leave your resort.

Disney's Old Key West Resort

Olivia's Cafe
$$☼ ☼ ☾ American

Olivia's has a basic menu with a slight leaning to seafood entrées.

Grovesnor Resort at Walt Disney World
☙B

The Grovesnor's *Baskerville Restaurant* hosts character breakfasts three times a week, and a murder Mystery dinner every Saturday night. Call (800) 624-4109 for reservations.

Hilton in the Walt Disney World Resort
The Hilton has a *Benihana's* and *Finn's Grill*, which is a great seafood experience. Call (407) 827-4000.

Wyndham Palace Resort & Spa in the Walt Disney World Resort
☙B The Wyndham has several great restaurants, including the *Watercress Café*, where there are character breakfast buffets on Sundays, and *Arthur's 27*, an award-winning restaurant that gives great views of Walt Disney World.

Summary

Okay, so there are so many dining choices, and now you have an idea what to go for, right? Then let's quit monkeying around with all the food stuff, and move on to what is important, THE PARKS! Let's start with the Magic Kingdom, and then see where it takes us!

Part II

Previewing the Parks

Magic Kingdom: Where Kids of All Ages Are Royalty

The Magic Kingdom is where it all started, at least in Florida. This park was established in 1971, but everything looks fresh and new along the storied Main Street, U.S.A. With crews that do nothing else but paint the buildings here, it always has a fresh coat, and the cast members always have a smile for you and your group. Many of the attractions are new and exciting additions from just the last few years. This park's rides do tend to be a bit more child-focused than those at the other parks, but there is still plenty of entertainment for guests of all ages. This is the epitome of what Disney World is about. Enjoy.

The Magic Kingdom is organized into lands that jut from the plaza in front of Cinderella's Castle. Traveling clockwise from the park's Main Street U.S.A. entrance, you encounter Adventureland, Frontierland, Liberty Square, Fantasyland, Mickey's Toontown Fair, and finally Tomorrow-land. The Kingdom is larger than you might expect, and visitors, especially those with kids, sometimes don't plan enough time to see all that they want to in this park. Make sure you leave enough time to visit all of the wonderful lands within the Magic Kingdom.

To do list

- ❑ Review the attraction descriptions and ratings for the rides and shows throughout the Magic Kingdom
- ❑ Mark the Magic Kingdom Trip Cards to plan your visit

Things You'll Need

- ❑ The Magic Kingdom Trip Cards from the back of the book
- ❑ Pen or pencil

Main Street

We all wish our home towns had a Main Street like the Magic Kingdom's. Designed after Walt Disney's childhood hometown, either side of the street is lined with classic storefronts, brimming with activity and friendly faces, and most selling Disney-themed wares. Main Street gets you in the Disney mood, as you pass groups posing for pictures with Cinderella's castle in the background. Savor this experience, especially if it is your first time here.

note Park HQ: City Hall, located just as you enter the Magic Kingdom, serves as your general needs information desk.

Cinderella's Castle

Basically just a home to a restaurant and a store, the castle is worth a walk through to see the tiled art on the walls. While there may not be a ride inside, a little time spent exploring the grounds around the castle is time well spent, and makes for an especially magical time for any child. It is, after all, the symbol of Walt Disney World!

note Feeling a bit shaggy? Well, tucked away on the right side of Main Street, U.S.A. as you enter the park is a barbershop. Some Disney veterans actually plan ahead so that they can get their hair trimmed here, which can even include, on request, some special sparkle or color additions for the day. The setting is nostalgic, the service is excellent, and the price is not too bad either ($17 for adults, $14 for kids).

Hidden Magic

Attraction Type: Experience Area/Playground

🚲 =5   🚲 =5   🛹 =2   🏍 =2   🛺 =1

🚲 = Ages 0-6   🚲 = Ages 7-11   🛹 = Ages 12-19   🏍 = Ages 20-49   🛺 = Ages 50+

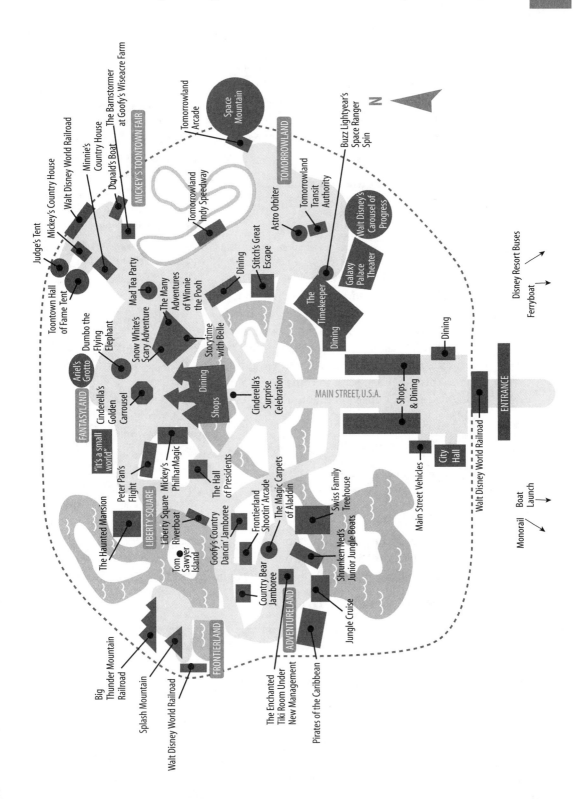

Main Street Vehicles

A variety of vintage vehicles, including horse drawn trolleys, take you up and down Main Street. Don't take these if you think they are going to save you time going down the street. They are an experience, and not a convenience.

Attraction Type: Carnival Ride

=4   =4   =2   =1   =1

"SpectroMagic" Parade

As with all other parades, Disney rolls out the characters to the delight of the children lining the streets. This is one of the better parades, as the nighttime spectacle packs the main avenues of the park. Every float, as well as the character costumes, is covered with literally thousands of lights. This is a great event to come back to the park to see after a nice afternoon at your resort pool.

Attraction Type: Parade/Fireworks

=5   =5   =2   =1   =1

Wishes Nighttime Spectacular

The fireworks at the Magic Kingdom have stepped up a notch recently, and while the best view is from the park, a close second would be from a boat on the lagoon, the top of the Contemporary Hotel, or the public areas of the Grand Floridian.

Attraction Type: Parade/Fireworks

=2   =4   =5   =3   =3

note Need a relaxing break from the attractions? Look around at the stores in the entry courtyard of Main Street, just as you walk into the park. As you enter, the horse stables are to your left. The stables are immaculate, and the workers inside are informative and friendly. The fire station next door also collects patches from fire departments from around the world, so if you are a fireman, make sure to bring an extra!

tip Don't miss these "Must-Do" activities at the Magic Kingdom:
Pirates of the Caribbean
Splash Mountain
"it's a small world"
Mickey's PhilharMagic
Space Mountain
Buzz Lightyear's Space Ranger Spin
Honorary Mention: Hall of Presidents

= Ages 0-6   = Ages 7-11   = Ages 12-19   = Ages 20-49   = Ages 50+

Walt Disney World Railroad

Okay, it is not a thrill ride, but this is one train that should be on your list, for a couple of reasons. The train goes all the way around the Magic Kingdom (clockwise) with stops at the park entrance, Frontierland, and Mickey's Toontown Fair. This is a nice, open-air, relaxing ride that gives your feet a rest and speeds up your exit from the park, as you avoid walking through the crowds.

Attraction Type: Carnival Ride

 🚲 =3   🚴 =3   🛹 =1   🏍 =2   🛺 =3

> **tip** **FP**
> The Magic Kingdom offers these FASTPASS Rides:
> - Space Mountain
> - Buzz Lightyear's Space Ranger Spin
> - The Many Adventures of Winnie the Pooh
> - Peter Pan's Flight
> - Mickey's PhilharMagic
> - The Haunted Mansion
> - Splash Mountain
> - Big Thunder Mountain Railroad
> - Jungle Cruise
> - Stitch's Great Escape

Share a Dream Come True Parade

This is the Magic Kingdom's signature parade, and seems to have the best representation of classic and new Disney characters.

Attraction Type: Parade/Fireworks

🚲 =5   🚴 =5   🛹 =2   🏍 =1   🛺 =1

Cinderella's Surprise Celebration

With frequent performances, this outdoor stage show is great for the aspiring princess in your crowd. Located on the Main Street side of the castle, the short show is complete with trumpets and fanfare as Cinderella is introduced to the audience.

Attraction Type: Theater/Movie

🚲 =5   🚴 =5   🛹 =3   🏍 =1   🛺 =1

> **caution**
> Be aware of where some of the disguised speakers are, as the start of the show could deafen you and scare the kids if you are standing in the wrong place. Look for stonework that is a bit darker. Closer observation should help you locate them so you can find a different viewing spot.

🚲 = Ages 0-6   🚴 = Ages 7-11   🛹 = Ages 12-19   🏍 = Ages 20-49   🛺 = Ages 50+

Cinderellabration

New in 2005, this replaces *Cinderella's Surprise Celebration* with an even more elaborate show that also features many more Disney movie heroines. This lavish show originally started at Tokyo Disneyland, and is sure to make every budding princess's day complete.

Attraction Type: Theater/Movie

🚲 =5   🚲 =5   🛹 =3   🏍 =1   🛺 =1

Adventureland

Welcome to the land of pirates and jungle adventure, home to two of the oldest and still most popular rides at the Magic Kingdom. Though little has changed at Adventureland, it's one of those experiences that continues to be fun as you grow older. This can be the best land to hit first because it sets your imagination going.

Pirates of the Caribbean

❄ The ride has basically not changed since its inception, with politically incorrect images of pirates looting and pillaging a Caribbean port town. And who cares? The fun robotic characters were the inspiration for the Johnny Depp movie from a few years ago, and there is nothing here that will make you blush, so consider the leisurely boat ride an air-conditioned must when you visit the Kingdom, if only because you have to say you rode it!

Attraction Type: Theme Ride

🚲 =4   🚲 =5   🛹 =4   🏍 =5   🛺 =5

note As you're planning your visit to The Magic Kingdom, remember how to mark the Trip Cards from the back of the book. If the attraction is one that you definitely want to ride, put a ✓ in the box next to the attraction; if you definitely want to pass on that one, put a ✕ in that box.

🚲 = Ages 0-6   🚲 = Ages 7-11   🛹 = Ages 12-19   🏍 = Ages 20-49   🛺 = Ages 50+

SHOPPING THE MAGIC KINGDOM

You may think that the shopping that lines the two sides of Main Street U.S.A. is pretty much the whole offering. But there are a few other nice surprises throughout the Kingdom.

* "Ears" to you! The most important shop, Le Chapeau, is just off the square as you enter the park. To your right is the store where you can get personalized mouse ear hats. Can you think of not getting your kid (or yourself) a pair of Mickey Ears with your name sewed on? Just $7 ($7.50 for adults), name included!

* Like Mr. Potato Head? Build your own in Toontown, in the *County Bounty* store near the Toontown Hall of Fame. You can select from the usual attachments as well as some Disney-themed ones, including potato-sized Mickey ears!

* Shopping in Adventureland is great, because not everything has a movie name stitched on it. The Pirates of the Caribbean store has items with equal appeal to 7-year-olds and college spring breakers, from eye patches to pirate hats to tie-dyed T-shirts.

The Magic Carpets of Aladdin

Fairly new, this carnival ride spins you around on cars that resemble the Magic Carpets soaring over the great Arabian cities. Yes it is just a carnival ride, but I think it has the best views, with a bazaar of stores and crowds of junior pirates sporting eye patches.

Attraction Type: Carnival Ride

🚲 =5   🚲 =5   🛹 =3   🏍 =2   🛺 =2

The Enchanted Tiki Room—Under New Management

This classic Disney attraction is one of my favorites, and it has recently been updated to make it even more fun. The animatronic bird show brings several familiar voices from recent Disney movies, some special effects, a great deal of humor, and some catchy songs to make this a fun sit-down theater experience that offers some fairly short lines.

Attraction Type: Theater/Movie

🚲 =5   🚲 =5   🛹 =3   🏍 =4   🛺 =4

🚲 = Ages 0-6   🚲 = Ages 7-11   🛹 = Ages 12-19   🏍 = Ages 20-49   🛺 = Ages 50+

Jungle Cruise

FP Since the arrival of the Animal Kingdom, it is hard to see why this is still such a popular ride. Why view animatronic elephants when the real things are a few minutes away? But the lines are still long for the boat ride through the jungle river setting that is more kitschy than realistic. I can't really say this is a must-do, or even something you should wait in line for, but if you are returning for the first time since childhood, or if you like a bit of silly humor, give it a try.

Attraction Type: Theme Ride

Swiss Family Treehouse

Crawl through the treehouse home of the ship-wrecked family, going from room to room high into the tree. Even though it is unlikely your kids ever saw this movie, it can still be a fun adventure (or an unnecessary climb, depending on your perspective).

Attraction Type: Experience Area/Playground

> **tip** If you are looking for an outdoor adventure zone for kids, opt for the *Tom Sawyer Island* in Frontierland instead.

> **note** Shrunken Net's Junior Jungle Boats gives you a chance to steer your own miniature boat through flaming torches, stone temples, and by other boats in this Adventureland locale. You have to pay to play, much like with the Frontierland Shooting Arcade, but it can be a nice distraction.

Frontierland

Keep heading around clockwise from Adventureland and you wander into a western frontier town. Get there early for FASTPASSES for either Splash Mountain or Big Thunder Mountain Railroad; the lines for those attractions get long very early in the day, and can become nearly impossible by afternoon.

Big Thunder Mountain Railroad

FP 🚶 Your train car is out of control, sending you careening through a dry southwestern mining town. This would not qualify this as a world-class rollercoaster on the scary scale, but there are plenty of thrills, and you can assume the standard

🚲 = Ages 0-6   🚲 = Ages 7-11   🛹 = Ages 12-19   🏍 = Ages 20-49   🛺 = Ages 50+

"should they ride this" rule for your group members as if it were a big-time roller-coaster. If you have a FASTPASS, it is well worth riding. You must be 40" tall to get on this ride.

Attraction Type: Thrill Ride

🚲 =0   🚲 =2   🛹 =5   🏍 =3   🛺 =3

Splash Mountain

FP 👫 Follow the adventures of Br'er Rabbit as your log climbs up this water flume ride for the wet and exciting conclusion to the ride. The child-oriented atmosphere should not make you forget that the drop could scare some kids, and that you *will* get wet (though not as wet as those on-lookers who stand on the bridge in front of the mountain). This is a must-do, assuming that the weather is warm enough to dry you off after the ride is over. You must be 40" tall to get on this ride.

Attraction Type: Thrill Ride

🚲 =2   🚲 =3   🛹 =4   🏍 =5   🛺 =4

Country Bear Jamboree

❄ This long-performing animatronic theater combines fun music, broadly accept-able humor, and a toe-tapping good time for all. If you saw the movie based on this attraction, I am sorry, but don't skip this attraction just because of that.

Attraction Type: Theater/Movie

🚲 =5   🚲 =5   🛹 =3   🏍 =2   🛺 =2

Frontierland Shootin' Arcade

You do have to pay to shoot, but the arcade is kind of fun. If you hit a target, it causes something in the scenery to light up or otherwise give you a show. And believe me, you don't have to be Wyatt Earp to hit one of these light-sensitive targets.

Attraction Type: Experience Area/Playground

🚲 =0   🚲 =4   🛹 =5   🏍 =2   🛺 =2

🚲 = Ages 0-6   🚲 = Ages 7-11   🛹 = Ages 12-19   🏍 = Ages 20-49   🛺 = Ages 50+

Tom Sawyer Island

This outdoor adventure zone loosely aligns to the story of Tom Sawyer, and offers an exploration for young teens and those just a bit younger. You reach the island by boat, and just because it is not an actual ride does not mean that kids won't enjoy it, so get off the ride-chasing rat race and let the kids loose for a while. The fort is just not to be missed!

If their kids are old enough to go unescorted, adults can wait at Aunt Polly's Dockside Inn in a surprisingly serene riverside setting sipping on a soda and giving the feet a rest.

Attraction Type: Experience Area/Playground

🚲 =3   🚲 =5   🛹 =4   🏍 =2   🛻 =1

Liberty Square

The world of the American frontier gives way to a revolutionary-era east coast city that mixes in the out-of-context fun of a haunted house and a riverboat. It just doesn't seem to matter that the decades get mixed, and open-air entertainment such as the fife and drum corps make it a lively area.

Liberty Square Riverboat

The riverboat is a pretty sleepy experience, so only hit this if you are in dire need of a rest. Of course, you could just go back to your hotel room, right?

Attraction Type: Carnival Ride

🚲 =0   🚲 =0   🛹 =0   🏍 =0   🛻 =0

The Hall Of Presidents

❋ Meet the U.S. presidents in all their animatronic glory. This stage show features animated, life-size replicas of every president, including whoever is currently in the Oval Office. This attraction is obviously patriotic, and while it may not be exciting, it is still a pretty good show. A stage full of 40-plus characters that independently

🚲 = Ages 0-6   🚲 = Ages 7-11   🛹 = Ages 12-19   🏍 = Ages 20-49   🛻 = Ages 50+

move and react fairly realistically is enough to keep your attention. While this is the same technology as the newer *American Adventure* at Epcot, the show is very different, so please don't pass it up!

Attraction Type: Theater/Movie

🚲 =0   🚲 =1   🛹 =2   🏍 =4   🛺 =4

The Haunted Mansion

FP ❋ Hop in a car and explore through this less-than-serious haunted experience. You really shouldn't worry too much about any but the most skittish kids, as the ghosts are more humorous that frightening. It is a bit dated, but is still well worth riding if you have the time.

Attraction Type: Theme Ride

🚲 =2   🚲 =3   🛹 =4   🏍 =4   🛺 =4

Fantasyland

When most think of the Magic Kingdom, this is what they have in mind. Princesses, castles, Peter Pan, Dumbo—all the classics. Fantasyland is now home to one of the newer and most popular theater shows (*PhilharMagic*) that is truly special, and it has several rides that may be designed for kids, but that most adults also find worth the wait. And when you see the little ones' faces, even if they are not your own, it will make your day.

Storytime with Belle

This small alcove brings your younger guests into a cozy story time with one of the more beloved Disney movie heroines. There aren't many seats, but if you need a break, this is a great place to get it, while collecting another picture-perfect memory.

Attraction Type: Character Encounter

🚲 =5   🚲 =5   🛹 =1   🏍 =1   🛺 =1

🚲 = Ages 0-6   🚲 = Ages 7-11   🛹 = Ages 12-19   🏍 = Ages 20-49   🛺 = Ages 50+

Ariel's Grotto

The grotto, which occupied the waiting line area of the long popular *20,000 Leagues under the Sea*, is under repair with a new ride coming soon. It is still a place where you can occasionally let your kids visit with Ariel, but don't count on it, as the construction may have changed the setting by the time you got there.

Attraction Type: Character Encounter

🚲 =5 🚲 =5 🛹 =2 🏍 =1 🛺 =1

Mad Tea Party

Hop into a tea cup that spins around madly in multiple directions. This is another Disney classic ride that is an almost required photo opportunity. It is neither exciting, nor high-tech, but the family that spins together laughs together.

Attraction Type: Carnival Ride

🚲 =2 🚲 =4 🛹 =3 🏍 =2 🛺 =2

The Many Adventures of Winnie the Pooh

❄ **FP** Travel through the world of Pooh, visiting all of his friends like Tigger and Piglet. This ride is appropriately tame for kids, but any adult that is a long-standing fan will enjoy it too.

Attraction Type: Theme Ride

🚲 =5 🚲 =5 🛹 =3 🏍 =2 🛺 =2

"it's a small world"

❄ Another Disney classic that has been recently refurbished, this boat ride lets you visit the children of the world, country by country. The song is infectious, and the scenery, while a bit 1970s, hits a high note in the nostalgia category. A must-do for all ages, simply because you have to say you rode this when you show pictures of your vacation when you return home. You wouldn't go to Paris and not see the Eiffel Tower, now would you?

Attraction Type: Theme Ride

🚲 =4 🚲 =5 🛹 =2 🏍 =3 🛺 =3

🚲 = Ages 0-6   🚲 = Ages 7-11   🛹 = Ages 12-19   🏍 = Ages 20-49   🛺 = Ages 50+

Dumbo the Flying Elephant

Sadly enough, some kids don't even know who Dumbo is, though they would have no problem identifying the ride if it were Nemo. Nevertheless, this falls in the same category as the *Mad Tea Party* as a great photo-opportunity ride, one that is used in most of the Disney TV ads.

Attraction Type: Carnival Ride

🚲 =2   🚲 =4   🛹 =3   🏍 =2   🛺 =2

Cinderella's Golden Carousel

This is a beautiful carousel, by anyone's standard. It is easy to see why most guests pass by it, feeling that it is nothing special that you couldn't find elsewhere. But if you have young children, or are a romantic at heart, you should take a ride and appreciate the amazing craftsmanship that went into building this vintage carousel.

Attraction Type: Carnival Ride

🚲 =5   🚲 =5   🛹 =1   🏍 =2   🛺 =2

Mickey's PhilharMagic

FP ❄ This has to be on your top five things to do in all of Walt Disney World. This is the newest of the 3D Theater experiences at Disney World, and it has taken full advantage of the technology advancements. The screen is wider than at all other 3D shows here, and the synchronization of the music, effects, and film make for an incredible theater experience. And if you are a Donald Duck fan, this should be your #1 stop.

Attraction Type: Theater/Movie

🚲 =4   🚲 =5   🛹 =4   🏍 =5   🛺 =5

🚲 = Ages 0-6   🚲 = Ages 7-11   🛹 = Ages 12-19   🏍 = Ages 20-49   🛺 = Ages 50+

Peter Pan's Flight

FP ❄ Soar over the world of Peter Pan in this long-popular attraction. Your car takes you from the rooftops of Old London to Neverland, retelling the Pan story. The ride is sometimes dark, but never too scary, and it seems fairly up to date, even though it has been a mainstay at the Magic Kingdom for some time now. This is a great ride for most kids, and is interesting enough for the parents too.

Attraction Type: Theme Ride

🚲 =5   🚲 =5   🛹 =3   🏍 =2   🛺 =2

Snow White's Scary Adventures

❄ This ride is similar to Peter Pan, in that you basically are riding through the movie Snow White. In this case, your car takes you by scenes from the classic, and while the name may say "scary," it is perfect (and captivating) for smaller children.

Attraction Type: Theme Ride

🚲 =5   🚲 =5   🛹 =3   🏍 =2   🛺 =2

Mickey's Toontown Fair

Toontown is a rare recent addition to the Magic Kingdom, intended to cater to the youngest of guests. All the attractions here are targeted to the tricycles and bicycles crowd, presenting a town, complete with an avenue of famous characters' homes, a park, and more. If you are traveling with young children, you will find this to be a true treat. Remember that the Railroad has a stop here, so you can make a fast exit from the park after visiting this area, if needed.

Toontown Hall Of Fame

❄ The Hall of Fame is designed specifically around kids meeting characters. It is a fun place to meet and greet, though the Judge's tent may better serve your needs if there is a specific character that you want to meet.

Attraction Type: Character Experience

🚲 =5   🚲 =5   🛹 =3   🏍 =2   🛺 =2

🚲 = Ages 0-6   🚲 = Ages 7-11   🛹 = Ages 12-19   🏍 = Ages 20-49   🛺 = Ages 50+

Judge's Tent

❄ The premiere character meeting area in all of Walt Disney World! You can choose from three lines, each of which leads to an area where your kids can meet several different, but usually related, characters. It is perhaps the best park locale for doing so, since the waiting line areas are indoors. The line does start inside a store, so beware the temptations of toys for sale!

Attraction Type: Character Experience

=5   =5   =3   =1   =1

Donald's Boat

Well it should be no surprise that Donald has a boat. Come on, look at his clothes, after all! The boat is a combination of a fun exploration area combined with a water park, all designed for small children.

Attraction Type: Experience Area/Playground

=5   =5   =2   =0   =0

The Barnstormer at Goofy's Wiseacre Farm

� A rollercoaster for Disney's smaller guests, there is still a height requirement, but one that many diminutive guests can pass. The thrills are in having a ride just for them, not in excessive speed or scary turns. If you have a small child, and they are tall enough, make sure they hit this ride. You must be 35" or taller to ride this attraction.

note Swing by Pete's Paint Shop to get a quality face painting for you or the little ones in your party. Located just as you enter Toontown, the artists are friendly and give you a good selection of painting options.

Attraction Type: Thrill Ride

=5   =5   =3   =1   =1

= Ages 0-6   = Ages 7-11   = Ages 12-19   = Ages 20-49   = Ages 50+

Mickey's Country House

Walk through Mickey's actual house, from the kitchen, to bedroom, living room, and all the rest. It may seem simple enough, but the attention to detail is both impressive and humorous. Many guests have commented that this attraction seems to make Mickey Mouse even more real to their children and enhances the magic of the whole vacation experience.

Attraction Type: Experience Area/Playground

🚲 =5   🚲 =5   🛹 =2   🏍 =3   🛺 =3

Minnie's Country House

Just as with Mickey's house, Minnie's cottage makes the character come to life for little children. It may sound silly, but just watch the kids' eyes, and you will understand.

Attraction Type: Experience Area/Playground

🚲 =5   🚲 =5   🛹 =2   🏍 =3   🛺 =3

Tomorrowland

Back when there was only the Magic Kingdom at Walt Disney World, this was usually the teenagers' favorite, largely due to Space Mountain. But while the famous ride is there, Tomorrowland has become a better mix of rides for kids of all ages, and the futuristic theme has been refreshed over the years so that it does not seem old-fashioned. With all the updates, many of our favorite rides are located here.

Tomorrowland Indy Speedway

👫 Okay, there are a lot of great rides here, but this is not one of them. Admittedly little kids love to drive around the track, if you let them feel like they are in charge. And with the track system, you can do that and not worry about anything, except keeping a foot on the gas. But loud cars moving at a snail's pace around a rail-guided track adds up to a pretty boring time for all but the youngest of guests. Hopefully the Indianapolis Motor Speedway people and the Disney Imagineers are

🚲 = Ages 0-6   🚲 = Ages 7-11   🛹 = Ages 12-19   🏍 = Ages 20-49   🛺 = Ages 50+

looking for a way to soup this ride up, because it is yawns-ville. To ride alone you must be 52" tall.

Attraction Type: Thrill Ride (barely)

🚲 =3   🚲 =3   🛹 =1   🏍 =0   🛺 =0

THE BEST DINING AT THE MAGIC KINGDOM

Sorry to say, but the Magic Kingdom isn't the best park for dining. But there are a few bright spots:

Best Overall Dining: *Once Upon a Time Breakfast* at *Cinderella's Royal Table*. This is the single most-sought-after seat in all of Walt Disney World. The setting is just too magical for anyone with kids in their group to pass on. You HAVE to reserve this 60 days before leaving on the vacation. If you leave making a seating arrangement until you get here, you will be out of luck. Check out the character lunch that has been recently added as well.

Best Full Service Restaurant: The Crystal Palace. Okay, it is a buffet, but the character experience makes it the best.

Best Quick Service: Pecos Bill Café. It has the best fixings bar of any burger/hot dog quick service restaurant in all of Walt Disney World, complete with nacho cheese, fresh lettuce, tomatoes, and grilled onions and mushrooms.

Best Snacks: Aloha Isle, in Adventureland. Dole brings some pineapple goodness here, amid a world of less healthy snacks!

Stitch's Great Escape!

FP 👫 ❄ Formerly known as the *Extra TERRORestrial Alien Encounter*, this attraction was softened a bit because the earlier version was just too scary for most. The attraction now puts you on the security detail watching Stitch, who naturally escapes and causes mayhem and havoc. The effects are fun, and it is far less scary, even though the attraction is much the same as the previous presentation. Be careful with some small children, as a prolonged dark period and some realistic effects might scare them. Guest must be 38" tall to enjoy this attraction.

Attraction Type: Thrill Ride

🚲 =0 🚲 =2 🛹 =5 🏍 =4 🛺 =4

Space Mountain

FP ❄ 👥 This is still the best known rollercoaster at Walt Disney World, and while the waiting-line décor of a space station is cheesy and dated, the ride still thrills. The dark interior lit only by stars makes the twists and turns a surprise, no matter how many times you have been on this classic. Guests must be 44" tall to enjoy this attraction.

Attraction Type: Thrill Ride

🚲 =0 🚲 =2 🛹 =5 🏍 =5 🛺 =4

Buzz Lightyear's Space Ranger Spin

FP ❄ At this attraction you are enlisted by Buzz to fight power-hoarding bad guys. Hop into a two-person car equipped with laser guns for shooting at targets throughout the ride. The guns actually score points for whatever targets you hit along the way, so you even get to compete with your party.

tip Quick hint: There is a target in the very first room to your left as you enter Buzz Lightyear's Space Ranger Spin that will score super high numbers right away. The orange robot's hand and the bottom of Zurg's first ship are worth lots of points, so hit them if you can.

Attraction Type: Theme Ride

🚲 =4 🚲 =5 🛹 =5 🏍 =4 🛺 =3

🚲 = Ages 0-6   🚲 = Ages 7-11   🛹 = Ages 12-19   🏍 = Ages 20-49   🛺 = Ages 50+

Tomorrowland Transit Authority

This ride is impressive, in that it is run by magnetic power, and technically has no moving parts but the cars themselves. You get an above-ground view of Tomorrowland, gliding around the park, and even inside of *Space Mountain*. It is not very exciting, but is a relaxing ride if you need a cool down period after a meal or before your next FASTPASS is valid.

Attraction Type: Theme Ride

=3   =3   =2   =2   =2

Astro Orbiter

This modern take on the traditional carnival ride has you circling on spaceships that rise up and down. Located in the middle of the courtyard in the center of Tomorrowland, it is a pretty simple ride with few surprises, but can be a good photo opportunity, just like *Dumbo* or *Carpets of Aladdin*.

Attraction Type: Carnival Ride

=3   =3   =2   =1   =1

The Timekeeper

❄ This 360° theater experience with Animatronic hosts is a bit more involved than the country pavilion movies at Epcot, but certainly is more for the youngsters. A bit dated, but it is another good show to hit if you are waiting for the time on your FASTPASS to come around.

Attraction Type: Theater/Movie

=2   =2   =2   =1   =1

Walt Disney's Carousel of Progress

❄ I am sorry. I really want to like this ride, due to its history (something Walt himself whipped up for the 1964 World's Fair in NYC), but it really needs either an upgrade or replacement. You sit in a theater that goes around to a series of stages with animatronic action figures that walk you through the technology advancements from the early 1900s to today. With the fortieth anniversary of the ride, it has allegedly been updated again, so if you need an air conditioned rest for a while, take a shot. Otherwise, you may want to pass it by. Let's hope that this is updated soon, keeping Walt's dream alive!

Attraction Type: Theater/Movie

🚲 =1   🚲 =1   🛹 =1   🏍 =1   🚜 =1

Galaxy Palace Theater

The outdoor theater is the host to an ever-changing list of entertainment, mostly musical. This can be a great rest stop with musical entertainment, but remember this is outdoors, so don't expect to escape from the heat. Check for show times and entertainment as you enter the park.

Attraction Type: Theater/Movie

🚲 =2   🚲 =2   🛹 =1   🏍 =1   🚜 =1

Summary

You have now been in the home of Walt Disney World. What next? Well, even after such a great time here, there is still so much more to see. So let's take a look at what the future and the rest of the world have to offer at Epcot.

🚲 = Ages 0-6   🚲 = Ages 7-11   🛹 = Ages 12-19   🏍 = Ages 20-49   🚜 = Ages 50+

Epcot: Bringing the World and the Future Together

Epcot stands for the *Experimental Prototype Community of The Future*, and it was conceived by Walt Disney himself. While it is vastly different than his original plans, the Disney Imagineers created a park that is essentially two parks, made into one. Roughly organized like a figure 8, this park conveys the excitement of the future, and manages to combine it with a view of the rest of the world.

Nothing is more fun on your first visit to Epcot than to enter by way of the monorail, coming from the Ticket and Transportation Center. The monorail circles Spaceship Earth, the large geodesic globe that is the symbol of Epcot, giving you a great view of the entire park. Spaceship Earth sits in the center of Future World, which celebrates different aspects of technology, nature, and mankind through a series of pavilions. These pavilions, which form a circle around Spaceship Earth, focus on topics such as the land, the seas, space, and our bodies. The pavilions take you on journeys that explore these worlds, and show how they will change as we, our technology, and our planet changes. This forward-looking approach makes it interesting and fun, and explains why they call it Future World.

In this chapter:

* Decide which future and world showcase pavilions to visit

* Pick rides and attractions that your group will find out of this world

* Learn how to shop the world, without leaving Florida!

I hear you. "Oh no, not *learning* on a vacation!" Don't worry; this is a fun park that just happens to have some learning hidden here and there. It has the fastest and newest thrill rides (*Test Track* and *Mission: SPACE*), a 5-million-plus gallon aquarium, and a lot more.

Then there is the World Showcase. This circle of pavilions brings different corners of the globe to you. Eleven national pavilions put you squarely in front of the Eiffel Tower, in the shadow of a Central American pyramid, or in the heart of a Moroccan bazaar. Staffed by students native to the many countries represented here, the World Showcase lets you feel as though you're globe-trotting. This part of Epcot brings some unique shopping, exceptional food, and impressive views. While it may not have very many traditional rides, the World Showcase is an experience not to be missed, especially around fireworks or meal times. It has been listed by many as a perennial favorite, simply for the great atmosphere.

So you have the whole world—and the world of the future—right at your feet. What are you going to do now? This chapter helps you choose which of the Epcot pavilions you'll visit, and it takes you on a tour of the rides and attractions available in each. This chapter also gives you an insider's guide to the best shopping sites available at Epcot right now—no need to wait for the future to enjoy this place!

To do list

- Review the attraction descriptions and ratings for the pavilions and rides of Epcot's Futureworld and World Showcase
- Mark the Epcot Trip Cards to plan your visit

Future World

Future World is based on pavilions that exhibit different parts of our present and future, including the land, seas, space, and imagination. These pavilions are also air conditioned, so you can cool down, find some interesting discoveries, and (heaven forbid!) learn something at the same time. Spaceship Earth sits in the center of Futureworld, and the other pavilions are then listed in a clockwise order starting to your left as you enter the park.

Things You'll Need

- ☐ The Epcot Trip Cards from the back of the book
- ☐ Pen or pencil

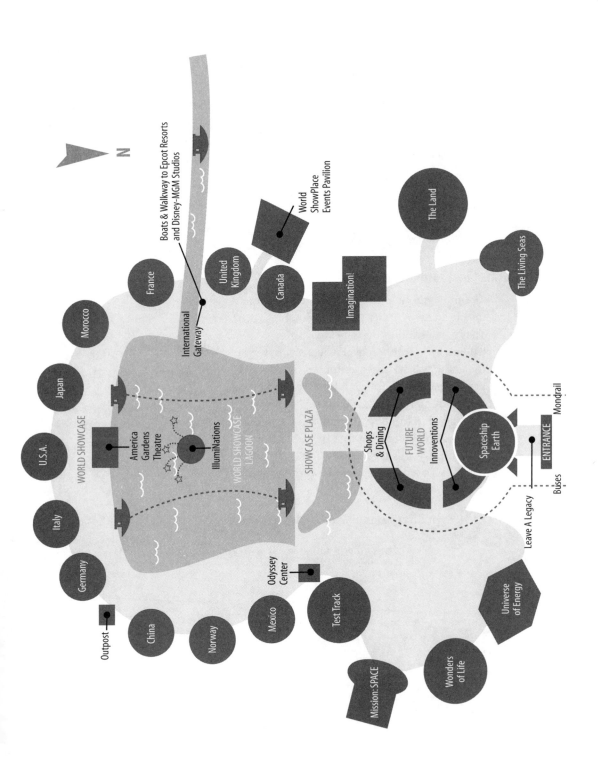

Spaceship Earth

✳ The white geodesic dome of Spaceship Earth is the symbol of Epcot, and all guests are sure to see it as the monorail circles the dome on its way into the park. Spaceship Earth recaps the history of mankind, and gives a nice rosy view of the future. The ride inside the dome is a bit dated, but still worth a visit during a day at Epcot.

note As you're planning your visit to Epcot, remember how to mark the Trip Cards from the back of the book. If the attraction is one that you definitely want to ride, put a ✓ in the box next to the attraction; if you definitely want to pass on that one, put a ✕ in that box.

Ride Type: Theme Ride

🚲 =2   🚲 =4   ✈ =3   🏍 =2   🛻 =3

Innoventions (East and West)

✳ Innoventions is actually two separate buildings located on either side of Spaceship Earth. They have exhibits designed to display leading-edge technology. Frequently, however, the exhibits have been outpaced by current developments, and seem a bit more like history than a glimpse of the future. Still, swing through on a hot day to enjoy the air conditioning, and you might find an exhibit or two that still registers a "WOW" effect. Also a winner if you have kids dying for an attraction that is a little more "hands-on."

note Ice Station Cool is a great escape from the heat, thanks to the super-cooled halls. Sure, it is an unabashed Coca Cola marketing venue, but you can try sodas from around the world and escape the heat at the same time.

Ride Type: Experience Area/Playground

🚲 =3   🚲 =3   ✈ =2   🏍 =2   🛻 =1

🚲 = Ages 0-6   🚲 = Ages 7-11   ✈ = Ages 12-19   🏍 = Ages 20-49   🛻 = Ages 50+

The Universe of Energy Pavilion

This pavilion is basically just the *Ellen's Energy Adventure* ride.

Ellen's Energy Adventure

❄ Ride with Ellen DeGeneres and Bill Nye, the Science Guy, as they discover the secrets of how we get energy today, and explore future power sources. Fun, and not too scary for the little ones.

Ride Type: Theme Ride

🚲 =2   🚲 =4   🛹 =3   🏍 =2   🛺 =2

Wonders of Life Pavilion

❄ This pavilion offers a couple of movies about the human body, a thrill ride that takes you inside a model of the body, and a central interactive activity area targeted specifically to younger children. This is a great place to go if you have small children in need of some interactive fun, or if the weather outside is rainy or hot. Kids can do some hands-on exploration with computers and exhibits that explain how the body works in very colorful, simple, and age-appropriate lessons. If kids aren't part of your party, this probably won't be part of the party either.

Body Wars

❄ 👫 You and your submarine are shrunk down small enough to enter a human body, and thus your journey begins. This simulation ride is based on slightly older technology, so it may not quite "wow" you anymore (especially if you were already on the Star Tours ride at Disney-MGM, which is based on the same technology). Guests must be 40" tall to enjoy this ride.

Ride Type: Thrill Ride

🚲 =2   🚲 =4   🛹 =3   🏍 =2   🛺 =2

🚲 = Ages 0-6   🚲 = Ages 7-11   🛹 = Ages 12-19   🏍 = Ages 20-49   🛺 = Ages 50+

Cranium Command

❄ This cartoon/theater attraction puts you squarely inside the brain of a boy, and you get a lesson on the basics of how the human body works. Really targeted at kids, but there are enough *Saturday Night Live* troupe member cameos from the 1990s to keep adults interested.

Ride Type: Theater/Movie

🚲 =3   🚴 =5   🛹 =4   🏍 =2   🛺 =0

The Making of Me

❄ Martin Short stars in this movie, which explores human reproduction and birth. There are a few sections of the movie where topics get a bit graphic, particularly with respect to fetal development. While the film handles these topics fairly well, you may want to consider whether you want your kids hearing such information at their age.

Ride Type: Theater/Movie

🚲 =2   🚴 =3   🛹 =2   🏍 =1   🛺 =1

Mission: SPACE Pavilion

❄ The newest of all Epcot pavilions, Mission: SPACE is not merely the home of the newest thrill ride. It also has activity labs and other exhibits that will make time spent here memorable and fun. These labs and activities are traditionally reached at the end of the ride, so make sure you take time to visit some of them (in particular, the video booth where you can send emails of your experience).

Mission: SPACE

👫 *FP* ❄ This new thrill ride has been an immediate hit. Mission: SPACE is a very realistic and exciting experience where you serve as either the Pilot, Engineer, Navigator, or Mission Commander. Each role has a different tasks, but the fun is equally enjoyable for all, so don't worry too much about jockeying into one particular role or another. It is important to note that you should keep looking forward during the ride, as looking to the side has gotten some riders a bit woozy (and even sick, as the vomit bags will attest) on the ride. Several NASA Astronauts were

🚲 = Ages 0-6   🚴 = Ages 7-11   🛹 = Ages 12-19   🏍 = Ages 20-49   🛺 = Ages 50+

reported as having said it was the closest experience to actual space flight that they had ever seen. Miss it, and you will regret it. Guests must be 44" to enjoy this ride.

Ride Type: Thrill Ride

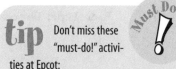

Test Track Pavilion

The Test Track Pavilion is basically the *Test Track* ride, with a General Motors-themed gift shop at the ride's end.

Test Track

FP 👫 ❄ You will have a hard time missing the rampant General Motors marketing everywhere, but it is at least something to read when you are waiting in line for this popular ride. Your test car gets put through the automotive proving grounds, complete with maneuvering, braking, and other driving tests, ending with a thrilling spin around the banked test track. It is fun, fast, and the end of the ride is a blast. Guests must be 40" to enjoy this ride.

Ride Type: Thrill Ride

tip Don't miss these "must-do!" activities at Epcot:
- Mission: SPACE
- Test Track
- Soarin'
- American Adventure
- Illuminations

Honorary Mention: Food may not be an attraction, but at Epcot it would be criminal to miss out on the flavors of the world offered throughout the World Showcase.

The Living Seas Pavilion

❄ This pavilion centers on a multistory, five-million-gallon aquarium that has everything from stingrays to dolphins and even a shark. In addition to the tank, the Living Seas Pavilion also offers a full-service restaurant, accessed from the right side of the pavilion.

There used to be an actual ride through this pavilion, but it is currently mothballed, pending a redesign. Nevertheless, this underwater sea base experience, complete with a simulated elevator ride to the ocean floor, is a fun and impressive oceanic experience. There are some Nemo-themed areas, including Turtle Talk with Crush and the Bruce's Sub House shark-themed play area. Also, if you sign up in advance

🚲 = Ages 0-6   🚲 = Ages 7-11   🛹 = Ages 12-19   🏍 = Ages 20-49   🚗 = Ages 50+

(and pay an extra charge) you can scuba dive in the tank, or swim with the dolphins. You can make reservations for these programs, Epcot DiveQuest or Dolphins in Depth, by calling 407-WDW-TOUR (407-939-8687).

Ride Type: Experience Area/Playground

🚲 =4   🚴 =3   🛹 =2   🏍 =3   🛺 =3

Turtle Talk with Crush

❄ This 3D, interactive theater setting is cozy and worth a stop for anyone with a kid. Crush, one of the characters from the Nemo movie, provides not only a fun theater experience, but actually talks directly to kids in the audience. Through some great Disney magic, Crush speaks to them, and reacts to their questions.

Ride Type: Theater/Movie

🚲 =5   🚴 =5   🛹 =3   🏍 =2   🛺 =1

The Land Pavilion

❄ This pavilion celebrates the lands of earth, focusing primarily on the role they play in feeding us. There is a significant food court here, a full-menu restaurant complete with a character meal, some shopping, a theater show, and two great rides. For more on your dining options, check out the Garden Grill Restaurant and the Sunshine Season Food Fair in Chapter 3, "Dining at WDW: The Real Magic at Disney World."

Soarin'

❄ 👫 *FP Soarin'* is a popular ride at Disneyland's California Adventure Park in Anaheim (known there as *Soarin' over California*), and so they brought it to Epcot. Racks of simulated gliders paired with a wide format movie screen take movie viewing to an innovative and exciting new level. "Soaring" above the ground, you will fly through a series of panoramic, breathtaking views of the earth. The ride is not particularly scary, but some children, as well as adults with a fear of heights, may want to pass on it. Guests must be 40" to enjoy this ride.

Ride Type: Thrill Ride

🚲 =0   🚴 =3   🛹 =4   🏍 =4   🛺 =5

🚲 = Ages 0-6   🚴 = Ages 7-11   🛹 = Ages 12-19   🏍 = Ages 20-49   🛺 = Ages 50+

SNACKAPALOOZA!

Frustrated that you can't eat at all the restaurants in each of the 11 pavilions on your trip to Epcot? *You can!* If you are traveling with at least one other person, try dining à la Snackapalooza! Start in Mexico, and work your way around, pavilion by pavilion, splitting a snack-sized tidbit from the walk-up food stands at each national area. Some suggestions include

Mexico: Nachos

Norway: Lefse (bread with butter and cinnamon sugar)

China: Egg Rolls at the Lotus Blossom

Germany: Pretzels

Italy: Gelati or Ices

U.S.A.: Funnel Cake

Japan: Tokyo Sushi Roll

Morocco: Lamb Shawarma

France: Crepes

United Kingdom: Fish and Chips

Canada: The seasonal choices are always the best!

Needless to say, these are just a few of the choices. Pick whatever hits your fancy, and if you are so inclined, you may also want to sample some of the specialty beverages from each of these nations as well.

Living with the Land

❄ *FP* This slower-paced boat ride may not be a thriller, but it is pretty cool to see how food can be grown in the extreme climates of the world. The hydroponics gardens in particular are interesting. These and most of the other exhibits are not replicas filled with props, but are creating actual food, mostly for the restaurants of the pavilion. This makes the ride more realistic and less staged.

Ride Type: Theme Ride

🚲 =0   🚲 =2   🛹 =3   🏍 =4   🛺 =5

🚲 = Ages 0-6   🚲 = Ages 7-11   🛹 = Ages 12-19   🏍 = Ages 20-49   🛺 = Ages 50+

Circle of Life

❄ This theater, featuring the cast from *Lion King*, shows nature's circle of life and how things we do can threaten that circle.

Ride Type: Theater/Movie

🚲 =4   🚲 =4   🛹 =3   🏍 =1   🛺 =1

Imagination! Pavilion

❄ The pavilion explores the human capacity for imagination, and all the things that it makes possible. Complete with a few different rides, a store, and an interactive lab area, the Imagination! pavilion is still widely popular, especially after a recent update to many of its areas.

"Honey, I Shrunk the Audience"

❄ **FP** One of the many 3D experiences at Walt Disney World, this theater show uses more than visual effects to bring the movie "Honey, I Shrunk the Kids" to life. The seats have water misters, motion simulators, and other devices that coordinate with the movie to make it come to life. Although that movie debuted in 1989, this popular 3D thriller has retained its fun factor over the years, and you don't need to have seen the movie to get it.

tip Here's a quick list of the FASTPASS rides at Epcot: **FP**

- Test Track
- Mission Space
- Soarin'
- Living with the Land
- Honey, I Shrunk the Audience
- Maelstrom

Ride Type: Theater/Movie

🚲 =4   🚲 =5   🛹 =3   🏍 =3   🛺 =2

Journey into Imagination

❄ The Journey into Imagination is an older boat ride that is designed to appeal to kids. This attraction explores our human senses, and how they play a role in our imagination and creativity. Although this ride is very slow and designed for kids, it

---

🚲 = Ages 0-6   🚲 = Ages 7-11   🛹 = Ages 12-19   🏍 = Ages 20-49   🛺 = Ages 50+

has several areas with loud noises and dark spaces that may spook more skittish children. This attraction may be boring for adults, but let's be honest, you mostly came here for the kids, didn't you?

Ride Type: Theme Ride

🚲 =5   🚴 =5   🛹 =2   🏍 =0   🛺 =0

ImageWorks—The Kodak "What If" Labs

❄ These labs, located as you leave the Journey into Imagination attraction, feature the largest digital camera in the world. While the post-ride activities at newer rides are more fun, these should still captivate younger children and give you a nice place to gather yourselves up before venturing back out into the summer heat.

Ride Type: Experience Area/Playground

🚲 =3   🚴 =3   🛹 =1   🏍 =0   🛺 =0

World Showcase

The World Showcase is a series of 11 international pavilions that encircle a lagoon. If you want to cross the lagoon, there are ferry boats that take you to either the Morocco Pavilion or Italy Pavilion from the Futureworld side. But with such meticulously accurate buildings, temples, and courtyards from around the world, you really should stroll around the lagoon, taking in all the sights. These national pavilions are a combination of both outdoor street scenes from the different cultures, as well as shops and other indoor venues, each seeming to sport an art or cultural display that changes regularly and is always seemingly ignored by the guests. Some are worth your time, so don't run by them just because they seem like "education" on a vacation. And if you can interact with the cast members, most of whom come from the actual countries, do so. They are enthusiastic ambassadors, and can make your experience more interesting, informative, and fun. The pavilions are listed in clockwise order, starting on your left as you enter the World Showcase from Futureworld.

note If you need a breather, but hate to think that you might waste some time at Epcot, try the boats across the World Showcase lagoon. You can rest, get a unique view of each pavilion, and cover a lot of turf all at the same time!

Take a Break

🚲 = Ages 0-6   🚴 = Ages 7-11   🛹 = Ages 12-19   🏍 = Ages 20-49   🛺 = Ages 50+

IllumiNations: Reflections of Earth

This nightly fireworks display is an absolute WDW "must-do!" While an illuminated video globe playing a montage of world scenes floats out to the middle of the lagoon, a pyrotechnic display complete with gas flares erupts in concert with a musical score. Get to the Rose & Crown Pub early to get a table outside if possible, or position yourself anywhere around the lagoon along the railings to get the best view. This is our #1 rated fireworks show in all of WDW, hands down.

Ride Type: Parade/Fireworks

Mexico Pavilion

The pyramid of the Mexico Pavilion is tucked into lush undergrowth; you'll feel as though you came upon it while walking through the jungle. Once inside, after passing the changing cultural display, you will find yourself in a courtyard, set under a permanent night sky. The Mexico Pavilion offers shopping, the San Angel Inn restaurant, and the ride *El Rio del Tiempo*.

> **tip** If you're looking for a romantic dinner site, the San Angel Inn is a great choice; read all about it in Chapter 3, "Dining at WDW: The Real Magic of Disney World."

El Rio del Tiempo

❋ This slow boat ride takes you uneventfully through a view of the Mexican culture. This ride is not very exciting, but offers a relaxing, air conditioned escape for anyone needing one.

Ride Type: Theme Ride

> **note** **Kidcot Fun Stops** are a great way to get your kids involved in the different national pavilions. Each stop gives them a craft to do. They are kept busy; you get to see the countries. Everyone wins.

🚲 = Ages 0-6   🚴 = Ages 7-11   🛹 = Ages 12-19   🏍 = Ages 20-49   🛺 = Ages 50+

Norway Pavilion

This is probably the most kid-friendly of the pavilions, complete with a Viking ship that they can climb around on, a character meal restaurant, a gnome statue and church ideal for pictures, and even an attraction ride. Don't miss the food, even though you probably never said "Gee whiz, I hope we can find a Norwegian restaurant!" The treats at the bakery are not bad, and the shopping is really great, though a bit on the expensive side.

Maelstrom

FP ❄ Another ride seemingly created by the host nation's tourism bureau, it is still a nice introduction to a country few in the U.S. know much about. It comes complete with an almost-thrill at the end. Again, enjoy the AC in the summer.

Ride Type: Theme Ride

🚲 =1   🚲 =2   🛹 =1   🏍 =2   🚜 =2

THE BEST DINING AT EPCOT

Best Overall Dining: Sorry, but it has to be a tie, depending upon your personal tastes. But some highlights include

- ❄ Restaurant Marrakech—Great atmosphere
- ❄ San Angel Inn—Atmosphere and authentic Mexican fare
- ❄ Restaurant Akershus—For the lunch buffet

Best Quick Service: Also a tie, but with the following recommendations:

- ❄ Sunshine Season Food Fair—For the best food court selections
- ❄ Kringla Bakeri Og Kafe for some sweets and best snacks

Honorable Mention: Dining outside at The Rose & Crown for the view of the Illuminations fireworks show

Read more about each of these restaurants in Chapter 3.

🚲 = Ages 0-6   🚲 = Ages 7-11   🛹 = Ages 12-19   🏍 = Ages 20-49   🚜 = Ages 50+

China Pavilion

The highlight here is the expansive store and the ongoing entertainment outside. From the Dragon Legend Acrobats to the Chinese harp of SI XIAN, the entertainment is captivating with a stunning backdrop. The dining is not bad, but since you can usually get Chinese food at home, many pass on the food offerings here. The shopping is extensive, especially for home furnishings and clothing.

Reflections of China

❄ This wide format movie offers some breathtaking views from across China. Another great movie that many miss.

Ride Type: Theater/Movie

🚲 =2   🚲 =1   ✈ =1   🏍 =3   🛺 =3

Germany Pavilion

No ride, just shopping, beer, and food. Don't get me wrong; that's a pretty good line-up! This is a great place to eat if you have a group that wants to have fun, especially at their Oktoberfest-like restaurant complete with band. This is a dinner reservation that an all-adult group looking for a good, loud time should make.

Italy Pavilion

Again, no ride. This time, however, the shopping has a bit of a more high-end selection than elsewhere, and some food and wine selections of interest. The courtyard tucked into the back is a nice getaway from the crowds, and occasionally has some fun entertainment.

USA Pavilion

This pavilion has two anchor attractions, the *American Adventure* and the *America Gardens Theater*. This outdoor covered theater has a constantly changing list of entertainment, largely dependent upon any special events that might be underway. Limited shopping is available, reminiscent of US national park stores, and there is also a Kodak kiosk. An important note is that this pavilion provides families the more traditional counter service foods (burgers, fries) that finicky kids who are not ready to take on the "tastes of the world" may prefer.

🚲 = Ages 0-6   🚲 = Ages 7-11   ✈ = Ages 12-19   🏍 = Ages 20-49   🛺 = Ages 50+

The American Adventure

❄ Built on the technology of the long-popular *Hall of Presidents* attraction in the Magic Kingdom, this theater-seating attraction takes that concept and technology a bit further. With animatronic characters and sets that explore great moments in American history, and advanced technology that adds more features to the show, the American Adventure is a must see.

Ride Type: Theater/Movie

$\overset{\text{\tiny 🚲}}{}$ =2 $\overset{\text{\tiny 🚲}}{}$ =4 $\overset{\text{\tiny 🛹}}{}$ =4 $\overset{\text{\tiny 🏍}}{}$ =5 $\overset{\text{\tiny 🛺}}{}$ =5

Japan Pavilion

This pavilion captures the architecture and spirit of Japan, but is mostly about the eating and the shopping. With no real ride involved, the Japan Pavilion usually offers an interesting display or art exhibit. But the real fun is in the stores, which are managed by a leading Japanese retailer. Complete with Bonsai trees, clothing, sake, toys, and even some interesting seafood snacks, the store is really a neat glimpse into current day Japan, and a good source for some truly unique gifts.

Morocco Pavilion

Like the Japan Pavilion, the Morocco Pavilion has no real ride. This is, nevertheless, one of the most exotic pavilions within the World Showcase, and one that may rank as the neatest to just roam through. The shopping is unique, if not as broad as that in the Japan Pavilion, with leather goods and metalwork. And walking through the maze of alleyways makes you feel like you are at a real Arabian bazaar. The real treat here, though, is the food, with Marrakech, a full service restaurant that transports you to North Africa. If you don't have the time or budget for full sit-down dining, grab a snack from the Marrakech counter service restaurant—you won't be disappointed.

France Pavilion

With the Eiffel Tower looming large in the background and great street theater in the front, this haven for stores and restaurants is a popular gathering place. The courtyard is also a great place for kids to get character autographs, especially those from the movie *Hunchback of Notre Dame*.

$\overset{\text{\tiny 🚲}}{}$ = Ages 0-6 $\overset{\text{\tiny 🚲}}{}$ = Ages 7-11 $\overset{\text{\tiny 🛹}}{}$ = Ages 12-19 $\overset{\text{\tiny 🏍}}{}$ = Ages 20-49 $\overset{\text{\tiny 🛺}}{}$ = Ages 50+

Impressions de France

❄ This is another sweeping movie, revealing the parts of France that you might not experience in Epcot's boulevards.

Ride Type: Theater/Movie

 =2   =1   =1   =2   =2

United Kingdom Pavilion

This seems like one of the larger "lands," complete with a fish and chip shop, a pub, and some back streets that have Beatles imitation bands and marching soldiers. The shopping is sparse, and not as high-end as it used to be, but any Manchester (soccer) fan would be thrilled. The food ranges from a real bar setting, to a sit-down restaurant, to counter service, with the beer selections being the highlight.

> **tip**
> Want to visit the BoardWalk? Use the "back door" for Epcot. That's right, the park has an entrance that leads to the BoardWalk, the Disney-MGM Park, and several hotels in the area. The International Gateway is located between the France and United Kingdom pavilions. You can select from walking paths and boats that are part of the Disney transportation system. If you are going to Disney-MGM, the boats are the best option; if you're going to the BoardWalk, walking might be a faster option, especially when lines are long for the boats

SHOPPING AT EPCOT

The shopping in the World Showcase is something of an attraction in itself. Kids can walk away with some fun, non-Mickey-branded goodies. Adults can get some higher-end products as well. Some of the highlights include

Mexico: Sombreros and other inexpensive craft goods
Norway: Gorgeous (but expensive) sweaters and active wear
China: Jade, toys, and clothing
Germany: Wine, chocolate, and cuckoo clocks
Italy: Wine!
USA: Patriotic clothing
Japan: Everything! Sake, toys, Bonsai trees, and much more
Morocco: Leather and metal goods
France: Perfume, wine, and berets for the little ones
United Kingdom: Tea, Wimbledon goods
Canada: Roots Sportswear

 = Ages 0-6   = Ages 7-11   = Ages 12-19   = Ages 20-49   = Ages 50+

Canada Pavilion

The last of the lands as you go around the lagoon, this pavilion is set back from the main walking paths, and can be a bit of a climb to really get around in the buildings and stores. But they are worth the walk, and the view from there onto the rest of the World Showcase is a nice surprise.

Oh Canada!

❄ Another sweeping movie, but Canada's formidable landscape makes it a good subject for this kind of show.

Ride Type: Theater/Movie

WORLD SHOWCASE ENTERTAINERS

The World Showcase has a variety of entertaining and colorful performers from around the world. These are just a few of the ones that you should check out if possible. Others are listed in the pavilions where they perform.

China: Dragon Legend Acrobats

France: Imaginum—A Statue Act

Japan: Taiko Drummers

Canada: Off Kilter

Germany: Oktoberfest Musikanten

USA: Spirit of America Fife & Drum Corps

United Kingdom: The British Invasion

USA: Voices of Liberty

Summary

So now you know how to see the future—and the world! Epcot has enough rides, food, and fun to keep you and your friends busy for quite some time. You now should have your Epcot cards all checked off and ready for that day at a park, so let's get ready to see what the magic of the movies has in store for you at Disney-MGM!

🚲 = Ages 0-6   🚲 = Ages 7-11   🛹 = Ages 12-19   🏍 = Ages 20-49   🛺 = Ages 50+

6

Disney-MGM Studios: Be the Star of Your Vacation!

Disney-MGM Studios is all about bringing the magic of the movies to your vacation. This park blends some of WDW's most thrilling rides with live entertainment that is totally focused on the kids. While the quantity of attractions may not quite match up with the Magic Kingdom, it certainly is the best balanced park in terms of having something for all ages.

While the park is about movie making, the entertainment goes well beyond that. You can sit in a TV game show hot-seat, live the fast-paced life of a rock star, and shop like you are on Rodeo Drive. Okay, the shopping is not that high-end, but it is some of the best theme-park shopping at Walt Disney World, complete with toys and more based on Disney movies. In this chapter, you learn how to find your way around the park, and you get an insider's guide to its star-studded attractions and experiences.

To do list

- ☐ Review the attraction descriptions and ratings for the rides and shows throughout Disney-MGM
- ☐ Mark the Disney-MGM Trip Cards to plan your visit

Understanding the Park's Layout

One challenge at Disney-MGM is that the park's organization is not as easy to follow as that of other parks. Instead of having worlds that surround a central location, the layout here is a bit more confusing, but nothing that you can't find your way through with a little planning. Basically the park is a set of "roads," starting with Hollywood Boulevard. This is the first "land" that you encounter as you enter the park. Think of the Main Street in the Magic Kingdom, but made to look like the shopping boulevards of Hollywood (thus the name!). As you emerge from the other end of this road, you are in the central point of the park, with Vine Street, Sunset Boulevard, Mickey Avenue, Commissary Lane, and the Streets of America all around you (see the map included here). These aren't themed lands; Hollywood and Sunset Boulevards look like actual roads from tinsel town, and the other three look like roads on the movie set back lots.

So with just a little planning, and you will be ready to hit the big screen!

tip Don't miss these "must-do!" activities at Disney MGM Studios:

- Indiana Jones Epic Stunt Spectacular
- Jim Henson's Muppet Vision 3-D
- Lights, Motors, Action! Extreme Stunt Show
- Rock 'n' Roller Coaster Starring Aerosmith
- The Twilight Zone Tower of Terror
- Disney-MGM Studios Backlot Tour
- Voyage of the Little Mermaid
- Honorary Mention: The Great Movie Ride

Things You'll Need

- ☐ The Disney-MGM Trip Cards from the back of the book
- ☐ Pen or pencil

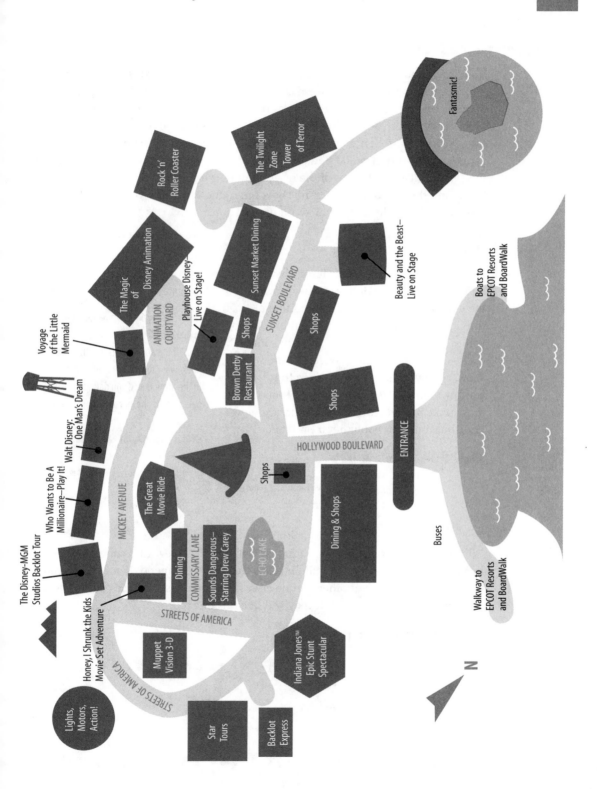

Hollywood Boulevard

Hollywood Boulevard serves as the Main Street of Disney-MGM, setting the mood for the park with a Golden Screen–era street scene complete with wandering improvisational acting troupes and store facades reminiscent of earlier years. Much like the Main Street at the Magic Kingdom, the Boulevard is packed with stores on either side, focused mostly on movie-themed clothing, toys, and collectibles. At the end of your walk down Hollywood Boulevard you are deposited squarely in the middle of the Disney-MGM park. One of the original rides is ahead of you (The Great Movie Ride), and the tip board displaying show times and attraction wait times is in this area, with the world of the movies all around you.

The Great Movie Ride

✳ See the history of the movies in this colorful and interesting ride. Hop into slow-moving theater cars that take you from era to era, through film's evolution from silent black-and-whites to today's blockbusters. Toss in some excitement reminiscent of Western film set shows, and you have a classic ride that is still worth waiting in line for. Some loud sounds may make it a bit scary for the youngest of visitors, but that's probably not a problem.

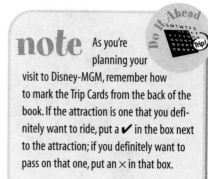

note As you're planning your visit to Disney-MGM, remember how to mark the Trip Cards from the back of the book. If the attraction is one that you definitely want to ride, put a ✔ in the box next to the attraction; if you definitely want to pass on that one, put an ✕ in that box.

Ride Type: Theme Ride

🚲 =3   🚲 =3   🛹 =3   🏍 =4   🛺 =5

Disney Stars and Motor Cars Parade

While the parade runs in more than just Hollywood Boulevard, I still prefer seeing it here, surrounded by themed buildings that really set the mood. Remember, even if your kids already saw another parade elsewhere, the classic vehicles and more than 100 characters will ensure that they will like this one too.

Ride Type: Parade/Fireworks

🚲 =5   🚲 =5   🛹 =3   🏍 =2   🛺 =2

🚲 = Ages 0-6   🚲 = Ages 7-11   🛹 = Ages 12-19   🏍 = Ages 20-49   🛺 = Ages 50+

Vine Street

Vine Street is home to some of the original rides and shows of Disney-MGM. As such, frequent visitors aren't as likely to flock here first thing in the morning, so it is not a bad place to start your day. The area has some restaurants and food stands, and offers a quick back way to get to New York Street.

These restaurants and food stands offer some of the best dining at Disney-MGM:

Best Overall Dining: *50's Prime Time Cafe*. It may not be fancy, but the atmosphere of being back at Mom's kitchen table is hard to beat, especially thanks to the incredible serving staff. Just be sure to eat all your vegetables!

Best Full Service Restaurant: *The Hollywood Brown Derby*

Best Quick Service: *Sunset Ranch Market*

Best Snacks: Turkey legs on Sunset Boulevard have attained legendary status with guests for flavor and portability

Honorable Mention: *The Sci-Fi Dine-In Theater*, because we all like to eat in our cars, even if we are not allowed to

Indiana Jones Epic Stunt Spectacular

FP This live stage show is a must-visit, as you learn the secrets of movie stunts. Since this is a show that occurs on a schedule, check times and arrive early (30 minutes on busy days, 15 minutes otherwise). That way, you can get a great seat (preferably in the center), and possibly be selected to participate in the show. Loud explosions could scare very small children if you sit too close, but otherwise this should be fun for the whole family.

Ride Type: Theater/Movie

🚲 =3   🚲 =4   🛹 =4   🏍 =5   🛺 =4

Star Tours

❄ *FP* 🚹 Get in on the excitement of *Star Wars*, with this simulated ride through space, using the same ride technology as *Body Wars* in Epcot. It is hard to miss the ride entrance as you pass under an Empire bad guy (An AT-AT Walker, for the Star Wars enthusiast) that stands about three stories high. The Star Wars theme

🚲 = Ages 0-6   🚲 = Ages 7-11   🛹 = Ages 12-19   🏍 = Ages 20-49   🛺 = Ages 50+

continues well throughout the attraction. The attraction seems a bit dated to regular visitors, but it is still a nice ride if you need to get out of the sun. Guests must be 40" tall to enjoy this ride.

Ride Type: Thrill Ride

🚲 =0   🚴 =4   🛹 =3   🏍 =3   🛺 =2

Sounds Dangerous—Starring Drew Carey

❄ This theater show has fun exploring sound effects; with the popular television star Drew Carey bungling along. There is a brief moment of darkness with louder noises that can startle children, but with a little pre-warning they should be fine.

Ride Type: Theater/Movie

🚲 =2   🚴 =4   🛹 =3   🏍 =2   🛺 =1

ATAS Hall of Fame Plaza

Not a ride, but a courtyard with busts of honored members of the film industry. Kids will yawn, but a pleasant spot for a quick break, especially if you brought your own refreshments.

Ride Type: Experience Area/Playground

🚲 =0   🚴 =0   🛹 =0   🏍 =1   🛺 =2

Commissary Lane

There are no actual rides in this area. It is the home of restaurants, advertisements for ABC television shows, and a quick pathway back to New York Street. The lane ranks low in scenery, but that's because it's wedged in between buildings housing some rides—and they do make it feel like you are on a modern movie back lot.

> **note** **FP** You'll find these FAST-PASS rides at Disney-MGM:
>
> - Indiana Jones Epic Stunt Spectacular
> - Star Tours
> - Lights, Motors, Action! Extreme Stunt Show
> - Voyage of the Little Mermaid
> - Rock 'n' Roller Coaster Starring Aerosmith
> - The Twilight Zone Tower of Terror

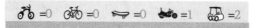

🚲 = Ages 0-6   🚴 = Ages 7-11   🛹 = Ages 12-19   🏍 = Ages 20-49   🛺 = Ages 50+

Streets of America

The Streets of America is a great area to explore, as it places you in the heart of New York City and San Francisco movie sets. You are surrounded by building facades, horizon backdrops, and prop vehicles that really make you think that an actual filming "shoot" could be going on around the corner.

Jim Henson's Muppet Vision 3-D

✳ A storyline that involves chasing a loose experiment created by Dr. Bunsen Honeydew brings Kermit and the whole gang together, including both onscreen and live characters. Make sure you see the Swedish Chef behind you (so don't get too settled down in that seat!).

tip Try to avoid the front rows, or the seats at the ends of the rows in the Muppets' 3-D theater. The seats in the center offer the best view of the action and the 3D effects.

Ride Type: Theater/Movie

🚲 =4   🚲 =5   🛹 =4   🏍 =4   🛺 =4

"Honey, I Shrunk the Kids" Movie Set Adventure

This playground of oversized household items puts your kids right into the movie. It also gives adults a great place to relax and have a soda, since it is next to a counter service food court.

Ride Type: Experience Area/Playground

🚲 =5   🚲 =5   🛹 =3   🏍 =0   🛺 =0

Lights, Motors, Action! Extreme Stunt Show

FP This is the newest attraction at Disney-MGM, and an absolute must-do! Your outdoor theater seating looks out onto a cityscape that soon bursts with flying cars, motorcycles, and more! The epic crashes, swerving bikes, and screeching tires are all at a safe distance; they are not on rails; and they are a blast to watch. Taken from the popular Disneyland Paris theme park, the choreographed chaos will wow someone of any age.

Ride Type: Theater/Movie

🚲 =3   🚲 =5   🛹 =5   🏍 =5   🛺 =5

🚲 = Ages 0-6   🚲 = Ages 7-11   🛹 = Ages 12-19   🏍 = Ages 20-49   🛺 = Ages 50+

Al's Toy Barn

Al's Toy Barn is a nondescript nook in one of the alleyways in the Streets of America. But if your kids are looking to meet any of their favorite movie characters from the Toy Story movies, this is the place to be! There is usually a sign indicating what character will be out next, and when. If you really want that autograph, get in line right away as it grows quickly.

Ride Type: Character Encounter

=5   =5   =2   =0   =0

Mickey Avenue

Mickey Avenue houses most of the truly kid-oriented attractions in Disney-MGM, including some really entertaining stage shows. But there are some things here for all ages too, so make sure you swing by this area.

> **note** If you are interested in a shirt or toy featuring a character from a Disney movie, this is your best first stop to finding it. As a whole, this ends up being some of the best theme park shopping at Walt Disney World, with a nice range of quality and price alternatives, and the toy selection is pretty impressive.

Playhouse Disney—Live on Stage!

❊ This show really lets kids get up close to characters, particularly the Bear in the Big Blue House and Rolie Polie Olie. They actually sit on the floor, just feet away from the big cuddly bear and his friends. Other characters from Disney channel shows are here, and if your kids like any of them, this is a great show for them. If it were not strictly oriented to young children, this show would rate as a must-do!

Ride Type: Theater/Movie

=5   =5   =2   =0   =0

Voyage of The Little Mermaid

❊ **FP** This performance is not a film, but costumed characters from the movie in a theater setting that completely submerges the audience to the bottom of the ocean. The cozy setting and action from all around the room makes it a true eye-opener for any fan of the movie, child or otherwise.

Ride Type: Theater/Movie

=5   =5   =3   =2   =3

= Ages 0-6   = Ages 7-11   = Ages 12-19   = Ages 20-49   = Ages 50+

Who Wants To Be A Millionaire—Play It!

❊ Ever think that you could have won it all on this popular show? Take a shot in this interactive attraction where you can work your way into the hot seat and play for real. Of course there are not a million dollars at stake, but win other prizes as you climb the ladder.

note If you want to find the popular children's TV characters Jojo and Goliath, you can often find their circus trailer outside the entrance to the Millionaire attraction.

Ride Type: Theater/Movie

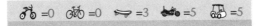

Disney-MGM Studios Backlot Tour

Must Do!

This is a signature ride at Disney-MGM, with most visitors familiar with the sights of exploding gas tankers and walls of water careening toward the tour cars. This ride shows you how stunts and effects are created for the movies. You can actually play a part in making some of the stunts. I did once, and while I got a bit wet, it was a blast being on camera and in the middle of the action. If they ask you to volunteer, do it!

caution Kids can be scared by the canyon experience, a.k.a. Catastrophe Canyon, in the Backlot Tour, so make sure that they sit in the middle of the car, not on the sides.

Ride Type: Theme Ride

The American Film Institute Showcase

❊ This is a regularly changing exhibit showcase, using movie props and other displays to bring a different facet or era of film to light. While it is interesting, you might have a mutiny on your hands if you try to take your group through there. Check the website for what current exhibition is in place.

Ride Type: Experience Area/Playground

🚲 = Ages 0-6   🚲 = Ages 7-11   🛹 = Ages 12-19   🏍 = Ages 20-49   🛺 = Ages 50+

The Magic of Disney Animation

✳ This is another attraction that could cause your group to rebel against you, but if you can get them to go, they will find that seeing what goes into their movie favorites is pretty cool. This is an especially great attraction if you have a young teen who is interested in art or drawing.

Ride Type: Theme Ride

🚲 =3   🚲 =3   🛹 =2   🏍 =3   🛺 =3

Walt Disney: One Man's Dream

✳ This exhibit honors Walt Disney and his vision for many of the different ventures of Disney. This experience is neat, even for the kids, as there are many of the original models for the parks, which still provide a "WOW" factor for kids of all ages. This exhibit won't be around for ever, and it is a hidden treasure that all should see, even if it isn't a thrill ride.

Ride Type: Experience Area/Playground

🚲 =2   🚲 =2   🛹 =2   🏍 =3   🛺 =3

Mickey Avenue Character Greetings

There are several different characters that your kids can meet here, with Sorcerer Mickey as the regular character. Again, the popularity with children of meeting the characters means that you need to get in line early to make sure that your kids are not disappointed.

Ride Type: Character Encounter

🚲 =5   🚲 =5   🛹 =2   🏍 =0   🛺 =0

🚲 = Ages 0-6   🚲 = Ages 7-11   🛹 = Ages 12-19   🏍 = Ages 20-49   🛺 = Ages 50+

Sunset Boulevard

Now you are in the Disney-MGM home of the big-kid rides! Sunset Boulevard walks you down the country lanes of 1940s California, complete with some open-air picnic areas and counter-service restaurants boasting some adult-sized turkey legs. Sunset Boulevard is home to the two biggest must-dos at Disney-MGM if you are looking to get your heart beating just a bit faster.

> **note** The picnic table outdoor dining area along Sunset Boulevard is a great place to take a break. If you packed your own snacks, break them out here and people watch. Also, you can wait for your FASTPASS at the Rock 'n' Roller Coaster or Tower of Terror to come due, or get in line for the next Beauty and the Beast show. And if you are really hungry, try the famous turkey legs sold here!

Rock 'n' Roller Coaster Starring Aerosmith

❄ *FP* 🚻 You are about to rock out with Aerosmith, but you have to get to the show first. Let's leave it at that, knowing that the "limo ride" of the attraction is perhaps the best thrill ride in all of Walt Disney World, at least for rollercoaster fans. Guests must be 48" tall to enjoy this ride.

Ride Type: Thrill Ride

🚲 =0   🚲 =1   🛹 =5   🏍 =5   🛺 =4

The Twilight Zone Tower of Terror

❄ *FP* 🚻 This ride exemplifies how Disney can really bring a story to life through attention to detail. From the moment you see the ride off in the distance, and hear the howls from the tower, to the moment you walk through the abandoned hotel lobby covered with cobwebs, you know you are in for a screaming good time. Complete with an elaborate plot and *Twilight Zone* clips, this ride gets your nerves ready for the free-fall drops that will either leave you getting back in line for more, or saying "Never again!" This is definitely not a ride for the little ones. Guests must be 40" tall to enjoy this ride.

Ride Type: Thrill Ride

🚲 =0   🚲 =0   🛹 =5   🏍 =4   🛺 =4

🚲 = Ages 0-6   🚲 = Ages 7-11   🛹 = Ages 12-19   🏍 = Ages 20-49   🛺 = Ages 50+

"Beauty and the Beast"—Live on Stage

The live stage show brings the movie back to life, complete with all the toe-tapping songs your kids will remember by heart. Beauty and the Beast is a really great performance—well worth the wait.

Ride Type: Theater/Movie

Fantasmic!

This huge outdoor amphitheater brings a nighttime show that showcases villains, heroines, and heroes from dozens of Disney movies. Featuring a stage that is a moat surrounding an island, this show follows a thin plotline as an excuse to parade different Disney characters by on boats against a pyrotechnics backdrop. With so much going on, it is fun for just about anyone, and scary for nobody. The Fantasmic Dinner Package allows you to eat at the Hollywood Brown Derby, or select other Disney-MGM restaurants, and have some seats to Fantasmic! reserved for you. Just ask the operators at 407-WDW-DINE (407-939-3463) if there are any special arrangements available related to this show.

Ride Type: Theater/Movie

🚲 =5   🚲 =5   🛹 =3   🏍 =3   🛺 =3

Summary

After your visit to Disney-MGM, you might be a movie star, a stunt man, or maybe a millionaire. With some of the most exciting rides and entertaining stage shows in all of Walt Disney World, your group is sure to find fun for everyone. You now should have your Disney-MGM cards checked for the big screen fun you are bound to have, so let's consider exploring the natural treasures of the Animal Kingdom!

🚲 = Ages 0-6   🚲 = Ages 7-11   🛹 = Ages 12-19   🏍 = Ages 20-49   🛺 = Ages 50+

Disney's Animal Kingdom: NâHtâZu (That's Right; It's NOT A ZOO!)

The newest of the major parks at Walt Disney World, Disney's Animal Kingdom, is a fantastic addition. Animal Kingdom combines traditional Disney fun with the experience of the world's leading zoos. As the newest park, Animal Kingdom still has fewer rides than other parks, but the ones they do have are some of Walt Disney World's best. In keeping with the jungle theme, the park's layout is unique; large Main Street-style avenues are replaced by jungle paths that wind through lush tropical plant life. Walking these paths can make you feel like you are not in a park with tens of thousands of other guests, but out on safari in Africa or Asia. The atmosphere of Animal Kingdom is a truly refreshing experience.

The park is organized into five lands, but to get to any of them you first have to pass through The Oasis. After taking any one of the many winding paths that makes up The Oasis, you will find yourself on Discovery Island, which is at the center of Animal Kingdom. The other lands are then organized in a circle around Discovery Island, starting at your left with Camp Minnie-Mickey, and as you go clockwise around you will find

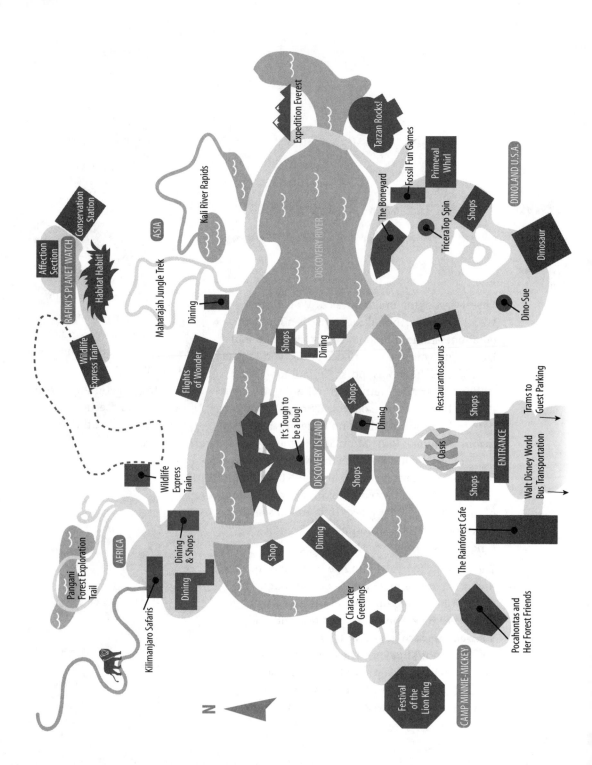

Africa, Asia, and Dinoland U.S.A. That's the order I've used to describe the Animal Kingdom lands and attractions in this chapter.

So get planning, because it's a jungle out there!

To do list

- ❑ Get the Animal Kingdom attraction cards from the back of the book
- ❑ Review the attraction descriptions, and compare the age-specific ratings that apply to the members of your group
- ❑ Put a ✔ in the box next to the attractions you don't want to miss; put a × beside those you definitely want to pass up

The Oasis

Okay, so this is not even a "land" at the Animal Kingdom. But you have to make your way through this area as you enter Animal Kingdom to get to rest of the park. Several winding jungle paths lead you by a variety of exotic animals from around the world.

Unfortunately, most visitors sprint past these natural treasures to get into lines at attractions elsewhere in the Animal Kingdom. While you too might want to rush past them to get your first FASTPASS of the day, you really should at least try to save the time to enjoy the exotic animals on your way out of the park.

Attraction Type: Experience Area/Playground

Things You'll Need

- ❑ The Animal Kingdom Trip Cards from the back of the book
- ❑ Pen or pencil

🚲 = Ages 0-6   🚲 = Ages 7-11   🛹 = Ages 12-19   🏍 = Ages 20-49   🛺 = Ages 50+

Discovery Island

This is the hub in the center of the park, from which you connect to the four other worlds and *The Oasis*. It is home to the symbol of Animal Kingdom, *the Tree of Life*, as well as to the park's largest concentration of shopping and eating facilities. Make time to visit the stores, as the wares here tend to be unique in Walt Disney World.

The Tree of Life

The symbol of Animal Kingdom, the Tree is a great place for exploration, as the body of the tree is a sculpture of hundreds of animals. Play with kids by challenging them to find the different "hidden" animals carved into the trunk and roots of the tree, especially during long waits in line for *It's Tough to be a Bug!*

Attraction Type: Experience Area/Playground

🚲 =4 🚲 =3 ✈ =1 🏍 =2 🛺 =2

It's Tough to Be a Bug!

FP ❄ This theater-seating, 3D movie is one of the better shows of its kind at Walt Disney World, and it is a must-see for older children and all adults. Be careful when taking very young children to *It's Tough to Be a Bug*, as some dark moments, as well as some of the surprising interactive elements with loud noises may scare them.

Attraction Type: Theater/Movie

🚲 =2 🚲 =5 ✈ =5 🏍 =5 🛺 =4

Discovery Island Trails

In the same spirit of the animal exhibits in *The Oasis*, these paths provide a casual and quiet viewing of some pretty exotic animals. Great for visiting if you are the part of a group sitting out *It's Tough to Be a Bug!* or after you have left the show.

Attraction Type: Experience Area/Playground

🚲 =2 🚲 =2 ✈ =1 🏍 =2 🛺 =2

🚲 = Ages 0-6   🚲 = Ages 7-11   ✈ = Ages 12-19   🏍 = Ages 20-49   🛺 = Ages 50+

Mickey's Jammin' Jungle Parade

Winding through Africa and Asia in addition to Discovery Island, this parade can either be a great experience for the younger members of your group or an opportunity for you to get into shorter attraction lines elsewhere while the large crowds are drawn away to view this festive procession.

Attraction Type: Parade/Fireworks

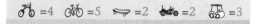 =4   =5   =2   =2   =3

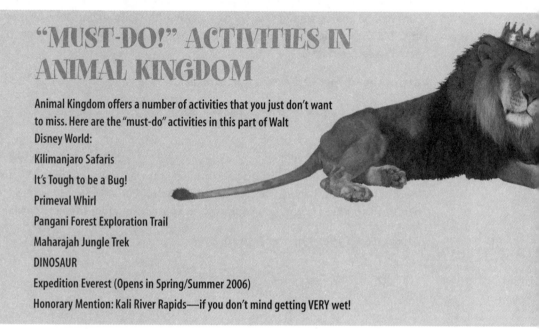

"MUST-DO!" ACTIVITIES IN ANIMAL KINGDOM

Animal Kingdom offers a number of activities that you just don't want to miss. Here are the "must-do" activities in this part of Walt Disney World:

Kilimanjaro Safaris

It's Tough to be a Bug!

Primeval Whirl

Pangani Forest Exploration Trail

Maharajah Jungle Trek

DINOSAUR

Expedition Everest (Opens in Spring/Summer 2006)

Honorary Mention: Kali River Rapids—if you don't mind getting VERY wet!

Camp Minnie-Mickey

This land is primarily focused on younger children, though the *Festival of the Lion King* is a pretty impressive live show that can appeal to all ages. Make sure you swing through here for that show.

Festival of the Lion King

❄This elaborate and colorful show is performed in a theater-in-the-round so all seats are fairly good (although the seats on the first row/floor don't provide a very good view of things going on at the rear of the performance). Vivid costumes and

 = Ages 0-6   = Ages 7-11   = Ages 12-19   = Ages 20-49   = Ages 50+

exciting acrobatics make the show fun for everyone in the family. The performance is in an enclosed theater and most characters from the movie are portrayed during the performance.

Attraction Type: Theater/Movie

🚲 =3   🚴 =5   ✈ =2   🏍 =3   🛺 =4

Camp Minnie-Mickey Greeting Trails

This is Animal Kingdom's site for kids to meet their favorite characters. It is fun for parents and grandparents, too, if only to watch the kids' expressions as they meet their big screen friends. Even though the Greeting Trails area is not a ride, be prepared to stand in line.

Attraction Type: Character Encounter

🚲 =5   🚴 =4   ✈ =0   🏍 =1   🛺 =1

Pocahontas and Her Forest Friends

This stage show, featuring characters from the movie as well as some live animals, teaches kids about conservation. It is definitely more focused to the younger members of the audience than any of the other Animal Kingdom theater shows.

Attraction Type: Theater/Movie

🚲 =3   🚴 =3   ✈ =0   🏍 =1   🛺 =1

Africa

Located near the back of the park, with the lands of Camp Minnie-Mickey and Asia on either side, this land transports you to the fictional town of Harambe, a rural outpost near the savannahs of Africa. Simply walking around this part of the park is fun, as vendor carts and other stores really give the feel of an African village.

Kilimanjaro Safaris

FP Get an up-close view of lions, elephants, giraffes, and many of Africa's assorted treasures. Both predators and prey are on display as your open-air SUV winds through the savannah landscape. You will be impressed with how Disney has

🚲 = Ages 0-6   🚴 = Ages 7-11   ✈ = Ages 12-19   🏍 = Ages 20-49   🛺 = Ages 50+

constructed the animal pens, making it seem that the animals are roaming free. All the while you'll be wondering how the animals are kept apart from you and each other. A thin plotline makes the experience seem more authentic, complete with a low-impact thrill at the end.

> **note** If you are staying as a Concierge floor guest at the Animal Kingdom Lodge, you can get exclusive access to a morning safari through this ride followed by a breakfast with your guide. Check with the hotel for prices and availability.

Attraction Type: Theme Ride

🚲 =5   🚴 =5   🛹 =4   🏍 =5   🛺 =5

Pangani Forest Exploration Trail

After you exit the *Kilimanjaro Safaris*, you get yet another chance to view some exotic animals up close on these walking paths. The gorillas are a must see, and all ages will find this trail interesting. This scenic attraction has more educational content than *The Oasis* or *Maharajah Jungle Trek*, but takes some time. Even so, it is a must-do!

Attraction Type: Experience Area/Playground

🚲 =4   🚴 =3   🛹 =3   🏍 =4   🛺 =4

Rafiki's Planet Watch

A land unto itself, this scenic attraction is accessible by the Wildlife Express Train taken from near the exit of the Pangani Forest Exploration Trail in Africa. There are numerous activities here, most based on demonstrating how the animals at Animal Kingdom are cared for and providing an education on conservation through interactive exhibits.

Exhibits include Affection Section (petting zoo), Conservation Station (which is air conditioned), and Habitat Habit! Maybe not the most exciting part or your stay in Animal Kingdom, but for younger kids it is a chance to pet the animals, and the educational part is interesting.

Attraction Type: Experience Area/Playground

🚲 =3   🚴 =3   🛹 =1   🏍 =2   🛺 =3

🚲 = Ages 0-6   🚴 = Ages 7-11   🛹 = Ages 12-19   🏍 = Ages 20-49   🛺 = Ages 50+

Asia

As you continue around from Africa, you are welcomed to the fictional Kingdom of Anandapur. This land puts you squarely in the midst of southeastern Asia, and is particularly reminiscent of Thailand. While Africa makes you feel like you are in the savannah, this place makes you feel more like you are in an Indiana Jones movie.

> **note** **FP** The following FASTPASS attractions are located in Animal Kingdom:
>
> *It's Tough to be a Bug!*
>
> *Kilimanjaro Safaris*
>
> *Kali River Rapids*
>
> *DINOSAUR*
>
> *Primeval Whirl*
>
> *Expedition Everest (Opens in Spring/ Summer 2006)*

Maharajah Jungle Trek

This is probably the best of all of the non-ride animal viewing experiences. The bat room is great but can be bypassed by those bothered or frightened by these little guys. While there are a lot of other interesting animals here, it is the tiger viewing that makes this worth the visit, as you are literally inches away from them, practically in the center of their pride.

Attraction Type: Experience Area/Playground

🚲 =4   🚲 =5   🛹 =3   🏍 =4   🛺 =4

Flights of Wonder

In this educational yet fun program, a variety of birds are put through their paces by trainers as you watch in an outdoor amphitheater. It may not stack up against the other exciting attractions in the Animal Kingdom, but it can be interesting and is a great way for parents to catch their breath.

Attraction Type: Theater/Movie

🚲 =2   🚲 =3   🛹 =2   🏍 =2   🛺 =2

Kali River Rapids

FP 🚻 Okay, it's time to get wet. A classic big-round-boat water ride, the themed canyon seems to make this fun voyage far better than similar rides found at local parks. Unless getting wet is a no-no, this is a must on a visit to the Animal

🚲 = Ages 0-6   🚲 = Ages 7-11   🛹 = Ages 12-19   🏍 = Ages 20-49   🛺 = Ages 50+

Kingdom. A change of clothes may be in order after this ride so consider tucking a dry t-shirt or shorts for yourself and the kids. Wet clothes may put a "damper" on the remainder of the day.

Attraction Type: Thrill Ride

🚲 =1   🚲 =4   🛹 =5   🏍 =4   🛺 =3

Expedition Everest

FP 🚻 Opening in 2006, this rollercoaster thrill ride is already a monumental sight at Animal Kingdom. Board onto a rickety train as you hunt the elusive Yeti through the mountains of Asia, but be prepared for the ride of your life. Certainly Animal Kingdom can use a few more thrill rides, and this should be quite a doozy when it opens up! Expect that this will not be a ride for the little ones, and that the FASTPASS system and height requirements will apply.

Attraction Type: Thrill Ride

🚲 =0   🚲 =1   🛹 =5   🏍 =5   🛺 =4   (Projected Ratings)

THE BEST DINING AT ANIMAL KINGDOM

The food is fine in the Animal Kingdom. Here are just a few of our favorite dining spots in this part of Walt Disney World:

Best Overall Dining: The character breakfast, *Breakfastosaurus at Restaurantosaurus*

Best Quick Service: *Flame Tree Barbecue*, with great BBQ, and scenic outdoor seating

Best Snacks: The fresh fruits at walk-up stands in Africa are a refreshing and healthy change

See Chapter 4 for other Animal Kingdom Dining Options.

Dinoland U.S.A.

This land's theme is that of a kitschy 1950s-era town populated by Dinosaurs. Sounds weird, but it is a great way to combine the still-hot dinosaur craze that kids love with a fun, tongue-in-cheek atmosphere that gives you a laugh. This is the land that proves that old carnival classics can be made cool again.

🚲 = Ages 0-6   🚲 = Ages 7-11   🛹 = Ages 12-19   🏍 = Ages 20-49   🛺 = Ages 50+

DINOSAUR

FP ❄ 🚹 A wacky scientist time-warps you back to the prehistoric era in a super-charged SUV to capture a peaceful dinosaur. Unfortunately something goes wrong, and you come face-to-face with a mean, hungry dinosaur instead. A scary ride for young children. Guests must be 40" tall to enjoy this ride.

Attraction Type: Thrill Ride

🚲 =0   🚲 =2   ✈ =5   🏍 =5   🛺 =3

Dino-Sue

Located next to *DINOSAUR*, this exhibit is little more than a replica of the recently discovered "Sue" dinosaur, the largest intact T-Rex skeleton ever found. Very interesting, and while it is a replica, the model provides a close look at one of the greater scientific finds of our times. So you should take a break from the rollercoaster rush to see it.

Attraction Type: Experience Area/Playground

🚲 =2   🚲 =2   ✈ =2   🏍 =2   🛺 =1

The Boneyard

This playground area actually has two parts to it. The first is like a jungle-gym on growth hormones. This playground is a great place to let the little ones loose, and it is well built and safe. The Boneyard itself is an even better must-see for kids. In this second part, they get to "excavate" bones that get reburied in sand continually throughout the day. As long as the weather is nice, this ranks as a must visit for kids, and a hidden treasure for parents to watch their kids explore.

Attraction Type: Experience Area/Playground

🚲 =5   🚲 =5   ✈ =2   🏍 =0   🛺 =0

Tarzan Rocks!

With songs right out of the animated movie and some fun aerial gymnastics, this live performance in a covered, outdoor theater provides a nice rest for everyone. The lines can be a bit long, but remember that it is filling a theater, so it moves very quickly when it is time for a showing. *Tarzan Rocks!* will close sometime in early 2006

🚲 = Ages 0-6   🚲 = Ages 7-11   ✈ = Ages 12-19   🏍 = Ages 20-49   🛺 = Ages 50+

to be replaced by another show in this theater. While word of the new show theme is not yet out, expect it to be a fun, entertaining presentation based on a Disney movie.

Attraction Type: Theater/Movie

🚲 =4   🚲 =4   🛹 =3   🏍 =3   🏌 =3

TriceraTop Spin

A dinosaur take on the classic Dumbo ride that has you flying in circles. Fun for the little ones, but just another line for everyone else.

Attraction Type: Carnival Ride

🚲 =5   🚲 =4   🛹 =1   🏍 =1   🏌 =1

Primeval Whirl

FP 👫 A fairly tame ride, but surprisingly fun. Sit in a round, spinning, roller coaster car that careens around short drops, twists and turns. Some little ones will be okay to ride, but let the more squeamish enjoy the *Fossil Fun Games* carnival attractions instead.

Attraction Type: Thrill Ride

🚲 =2   🚲 =3   🛹 =4   🏍 =4   🏌 =5

Fossil Fun Games

Carnival games with a dinosaur theme, and no creepy carnies to spook you. This is a great place for those who are sitting out either the *Primeval Whirl* or *TriceraTop Spin*.

Attraction Type: Experience Area/Playground

🚲 =3   🚲 =3   🛹 =2   🏍 =1   🏌 =1

🚲 = Ages 0-6   🚲 = Ages 7-11   🛹 = Ages 12-19   🏍 = Ages 20-49   🏌 = Ages 50+

Cretaceous Trail

This trail, like the *Pangani Forest Exploration Trail* and *Maharajah Jungle Trek*, gives you an up-close view of a variety of animals. But unlike the other trails, this one's residents aren't actually alive—they are animatronic models of dinosaurs. Kids will love it, and will actually learn something.

Attraction Type: Experience Area/Playground

Summary

You have now seen animals from the corners of the world, and even from our past. What could possibly beat this wild safari of a theme park day? Well, you could go see wildlife of another sort at one of Walt Disney World's nightlife areas. See the youngsters howl at the moon in the hopping nightclubs of Pleasure Island or hold hands with your sweetheart in the light of the moon as you walk along a 1930s era BoardWalk.

Part III

The Rest of the Kingdom

Disney After Dark: Downtown Disney and BoardWalk

8

In this chapter:

* Review the shopping and dining options at Downtown Disney, and learn where to find the best kid-friendly or adults-only entertainment in the area.

* Learn about the shopping, dining, and crowd-entertaining shops and activities at Disney's BoardWalk

Many people who visited the Magic Kingdom in the '70s or '80s still believe that Walt Disney World doesn't offer adult-oriented fun. But times have changed, and nothing could be further from the truth. Disney has not just tried to make a parent's time more fun, it's also tried to make the park a destination for adult-only groups. The Disney nightlife may not be as thrilling as the club scene in LA, but Walt Disney World has taken steps to keep guests of all ages entertained in the evening hours.

So what is there to do? The selection of restaurants certainly has improved. Evenings in the World Showcase at Epcot are also a great escape combining fireworks, food, drink, and shopping. But this chapter is all about two very different experiences that Disney has assembled to open up your fun side (and your wallet!) in the evening hours. At Downtown Disney and on the BoardWalk, Disney has assembled food, entertainment, and shopping that will give you a reason to make more out of your evenings than you might have imagined. The motto of Downtown Disney really captures it. *Carpe PM*—seize the night!

To do list

- ❑ Decide which areas of Downtown Disney you want to visit and when
- ❑ List the stores and entertainment you want to visit in the West Side, Pleasure Island, and Marketplace
- ❑ Make Advanced Reservation arrangements for any meals

Downtown Disney

Long ago, Walt Disney World had a little-visited shopping area called Lake Buena Vista where you could pick up some basic groceries and maybe a Mickey T-shirt. Over time, Disney has expanded this area greatly into a shopping, restaurant, and nightclub complex. Now known as Downtown Disney, it is split into three distinct areas, West Side, Pleasure Island, and the Marketplace, each offering a different kind of distraction. While it may have its limitations, the area has certainly expanded to the point that most groups visiting Walt Disney World could find at least one or two reasons why they would want to include it on their vacation planning. So let's look at these three areas, going from left to right as you approach them from the parking area.

Things You'll Need

- ❑ Your General Information Trip Cards
- ❑ Pen or pencil

MUST DO! AT DOWNTOWN DISNEY

Mannequins Dance Palace

Adventurer's Club

Cirque du Soleil

World of Disney

The Art of Disney/Wonderful World of Memories

Basin

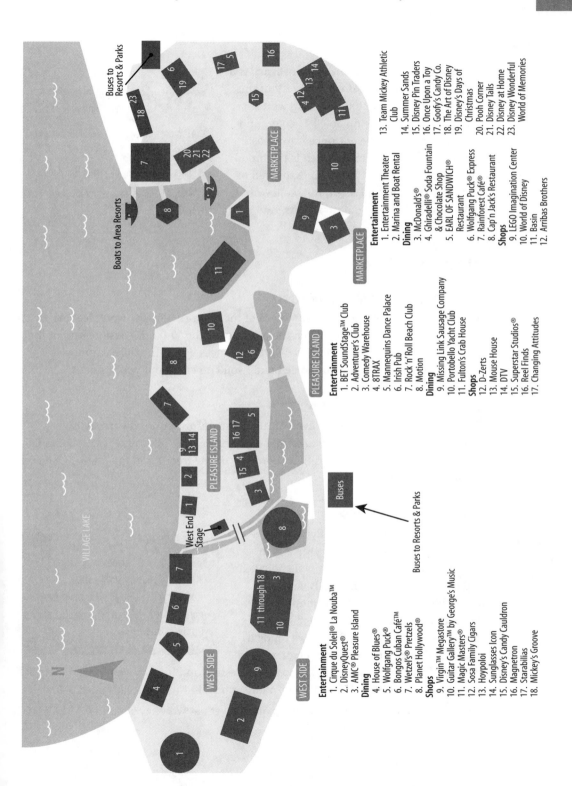

WEST SIDE

Entertainment
1. Cirque du Soleil® La Nouba™
2. DisneyQuest®
3. AMC® Pleasure Island

Dining
4. House of Blues®
5. Wolfgang Puck®
6. Bongos Cuban Café™
7. Wetzel's® Pretzels
8. Planet Hollywood®

Shops
9. Virgin™ Megastore
10. Guitar Gallery™ by George's Music
11. Magic Masters®
12. Sosa Family Cigars
13. Hoypoloi
14. Sunglasses Icon
15. Disney's Candy Cauldron
16. Magnetron
17. Starabilias
18. Mickey's Groove

PLEASURE ISLAND

Entertainment
1. BET SoundStage™ Club
2. Adventurer's Club
3. Comedy Warehouse
4. 8TRAX
5. Mannequins Dance Palace
6. Irish Pub
7. Rock 'n' Roll Beach Club
8. Motion

Dining
9. Missing Link Sausage Company
10. Portobello Yacht Club
11. Fulton's Crab House

Shops
12. D-Zerts
13. Mouse House
14. DTV
15. Superstar Studios®
16. Reel Finds
17. Changing Attitudes

MARKETPLACE

Entertainment
1. Entertainment Theater
2. Marina and Boat Rental

Dining
3. McDonald's®
4. Ghiradelli® Soda Fountain & Chocolate Shop
5. EARL OF SANDWICH® Restaurant
6. Wolfgang Puck® Express
7. Rainforest Café®
8. Cap'n Jack's Restaurant

Shops
9. LEGO Imagination Center
10. World of Disney
11. Basin
12. Arribas Brothers
13. Team Mickey Athletic Club
14. Summer Sands
15. Disney Pin Traders
16. Once Upon a Toy
17. Goofy's Candy Co.
18. The Art of Disney
19. Disney's Days of Christmas
20. Pooh Corner
21. Disney Tails
22. Disney at Home
23. Disney Wonderful World of Memories

West Side

The West Side section of Downtown Disney is a broad walking street of stores and restaurants anchored at one end by the soaring white structure of the Cirque du Soleil Theater, and at the other end by the entrance into Pleasure Island. The real draw in this area is the broad array of trendy and exotic cuisines, as well as the fun of just strolling along the boulevard peeking into stores for guitars, cigars, and movie memorabilia.

note Keep this information in mind during your visit:

- ATMs are located by Wetzel's Pretzels and House of Blues
- Buses are available by Planet Hollywood
- West Side stores and restaurants start opening around 11:00 a.m.

Entertainment/Dining

AMC Pleasure Island Movie Theaters

With 24 theaters, even a rainy day crowd of theme park refugees won't feel too crowded. Entrances are across from the entrance of the Virgin Megastore and at the Pleasure Island end of the West Side. Both entrances list all the different movies being shown, so if you need a movie break, you can check out your options.

Bongos Cuban Café

This Gloria and Emilio Estefan-owned Cuban restaurant brings a very stylish Miami/Caribbean atmosphere to dinner and drinks. The Cuban fare offers some flavorful but not too spicy choices that should be a new treat for many guests. Open for lunch and dinner.

Cirque du Soleil La Nouba

Any fan of this troupe's high-flying, new age theatrics should make sure to visit this show. Anyone not familiar with Cirque du Soleil can find out more at www.cirquedusoleil.com about this troupe whose performances are a fusion of circus acrobatics, theater, art, and music. Certainly unique, they have made a name for themselves by creating esoteric and

note If you are planning on attending Cirque du Soleil, make sure that you call ahead for seating reservations. It may have been here a while, but it is still a popular show.

exotic performances that combine some impressive and innovative physical feats of skill. Prices range from $59 to $87 for adults, and $44 to $65 for kids aged 3–9.

For tickets, you can buy online at www.omniticket.net/wdwcds, or call 407-939-7719.

DisneyQuest Indoor Interactive Theme Park

Several years ago, Disney was looking for a way to bring the fun of a theme park to cities where the weather did not want to cooperate. Many of these indoor parks, like the one in downtown Chicago, have closed. But the one at Walt Disney World is still open, and it is a great place to go on a rainy day, or in the evening with kids. This multi-floor entertainment venue combines advanced computer technologies to guide guests through a variety of "rides," including one in which you build your own rollercoaster then ride it via a virtual reality simulator. The park includes a fast-food restaurant. Prices are $34 for adults, and $28 for kids aged 3–9. When purchasing tickets for the theme parks, consider adding the *Magic Plus Pack Option* that would include admission to DisneyQuest (See Chapter 1, "Planning Your Walt Disney World Trip"). DisneyQuest is usually open from 11:30 a.m. until 11:00 p.m.

> **note** See Chapter 3, "Dining at WDW: The Real Magic of Disney World," for full reviews of the restaurants mentioned in this chapter.

House of Blues Bar and Restaurant

This bar/restaurant is part of the popular chain, and offers some great live music, as well as a vibrant bar scene. The store in the front of the building offers related merchandise, and more than a few visitors have recommended the Gospel Brunch on Sundays. Open for lunch and dinner. See Chapter 3 for a review of this and other restaurants.

Planet Hollywood Restaurant

Planet Hollywood is at the opposite end of West Side from the Cirque du Soleil Theater. The restaurant's large blue globe is a sight in itself. Inside, you can select from a wide range of entrées for lunch or dinner. A store on the West Side strip sells related merchandise.

Wetzel's Pretzels

This fast-food service restaurant offers (surprise) pretzels, as well as several other fast-food selections that you can carry around with you to make that hunger pang subside. Think of this as a good place to quell your hunger while you wait for your table at one of the many restaurants in the area, as well as lowering your restaurant bill by skipping the appetizer course at the more expensive restaurant. See Chapter 3 for a review of this and other restaurants.

Wolfgang Puck Restaurants

Wolfgang has provided four restaurants in one, including an express window for some quicker foods, a sushi bar/lounge, a casual but date-worthy moderately priced full service restaurant called The Café, and an upscale, high ticket special event experience on the top floor. The Café is one of our favorites, for the food and the value, and the express window is also a favorite for a sandwich on the go. Open for lunch and dinner.

Shopping

Disney's Candy Cauldron

Like you weren't already eating enough sugar on this vacation, and now you are faced with every color of M&M you could ever desire. Come in to watch them make some of their chocolate and sugar coated goodies, and walk out with a bag full of dessert that you can all share. And you were so proud that you turned down dessert at dinner, weren't you?

Guitar Gallery by George's Music

I am not a guitar player, so I can't speak to the quality of the products in this store. Suffice it to say, it certainly *looks* like a true music aficionado's kind of store, with a variety of acoustic and electric guitars, accessories, and other goodies worth investigating.

Hoypoloi Gallery

A broad array of vibrant art, almost exclusively contemporary, shows you that not *everything* for sale at Walt Disney World has Mickey ears tattooed on it. Of course, carrying around a glass sculpture throughout the rest of the evening could be annoying, so ask about the gallery's shipping services.

Magic Masters Magic Store

This small storefront has a magician hard at work, entertaining a small crowd of customers with different tricks with the hopes of making them change into customers with the wave of a wand. Don't ask him what the secret is behind the tricks—that is what he is trying to sell you! I have been convinced more than once to buy, and I have never been disappointed.

Magnetron Gift Shop

This store dedicated to magnets would make any refrigerator door shudder! I know what you are thinking: Why would I care about refrigerator magnets? But I can guarantee that the selection in this store gives you a chance to find your next kitchen conversation piece, and it is a lot less expensive than buying a new food processor.

Mickey's Groove Gift Shop

This store has a nice selection of Disney stuff, but if you are planning on spending any time at the stores at the Marketplace area, it is unlikely that you are going to find anything here of much interest.

Sosa Family Cigars

With a store here and in the Marketplace end of Downtown Disney, cigar smokers have two chances to stock up on some of their favorite stogies. The scents that pour out of the storefront would draw even an infrequent cigar fan in, and the store's comfortable seating area will beg you to stay and enjoy one of your purchases.

Starabilias Movie Memorabilia

The array of movie, television, and other autographed memorabilia is pretty impressive. The collection of actual costumes, vintage photographs, movie posters, sports gear, and more, usually autographed, would give any collector a great distraction for at least 15 minutes. And of course it is all for sale—at a price.

Sunglasses Icon

Vacations can be murder on sunglasses, and this is the best place to replace that lost or crushed set that you brought with you from home. Prices can get pretty steep, but you should be able to find something in your range, at least for an adult.

Virgin Megastore

The music selection on the first floor of this gigantic media store is impressive. The book selection has dwindled quite a bit, but it is still the best place in all of Walt Disney World to get that poolside read that you might have forgotten to pack.

Pleasure Island

Disney created Pleasure Island to provide a true nightclub environment where adults could enjoy themselves in the evenings. This is basically a long walking street with clubs, drink stands, and stores on either side of the street, with the end nearest the West Side featuring a large, open-air bandstand. Every evening around midnight, all year long, they celebrate a New-Year's-Eve-like countdown from the bandstand.

While Disney is trying to create a nightclub environment, but guests of any age can stroll down the walking street. And guests of any age can also get into most of the clubs if they have purchased a club admission ticket. The $16.95 (plus 6% tax) admission to the Pleasure Island clubs can be part of your theme park admission tickets, if you purchase the *Magic Plus Pack* Option (see Chapter 1).

The admission of all ages into Pleasure Island creates an environment where you could be in a club, enjoying a cocktail, while some six-year-old is behind you having a major temper tantrum. Worse yet, you could bring your kids and have them encounter rowdy drunks, whooping it up. Certainly the "adult" atmosphere of the Island has a tainted feel to it. There are two clubs (Mannequins and BET Soundstage) that limit admission to their clubs from Thursday to Sunday to just 21-year-olds and older, but for the rest of the clubs, you have to be prepared for kids to be nearby.

So that you don't think I am putting this place down, many guests have had some great memories here. It is a fun place to go with a group of adults, and there is a club for many different moods, musical tastes, and groups. The dance floors fill up for a fun, safe time, the restrooms are a great deal cleaner than at the average bar, and there is something about Pleasure Island that is especially convenient— a bus back to your resort means no drunk driving.

> **note** Here are a few points to remember during your visit to Pleasure Island:
>
> - Lockers and an ATM are located by the Rock 'n' Roll Beach Club
> - Pleasure Island is usually open from 7:00 p.m. to 2:00 a.m.
> - Buses are made available by Planet Hollywood
> - Smoking is not allowed in any of the clubs
> - Admission to Pleasure Island can be a part of your Walt Disney World tickets with the purchase of the Magic Plus Pack Option on your theme park tickets

Entertainment/Dining

8TRAX

'70s and '80s tunes in a retro dance club that will make anyone who grew up in this era chuckle. The big screens throughout this small club run videos and TV shows from the '80s, and you might be reminded of just how bad your taste was back then. If you like music from this era, it is a must visit!

Adventurer's Club

The Adventurer's Club is what one would expect of a Disney-run nightclub. Enter and you are dropped into a cartoonish rendition of a British colonial-era men's club complete with actors who roam around interacting with the guests. There are entertaining tales told in several different rooms where PG-13-rated stories delivered by Indiana Jones-style adventurers, debutantes, and a British colonial officer keep the guests laughing. Many would recommend that you try the syrupy Kungaloosh cocktail that is the namesake of the club's oath of membership, but I recommend the Pamalia's Punch.

BET SoundStage Club

This Black Entertainment Television–sponsored dance club is a cool, sleek joint that plays rap, hip-hop, and other contemporary music. Multiple levels overlook the dance floor, and there is a great scenic view of Village Lake out the back of the club. This may be one of your top club choices here, especially if you like these genres of music.

Comedy Warehouse

The comedy here is not 100% Disney content, so it can get a bit racy every now and then. If you have kids, you might think twice about bringing them to this club. It certainly isn't loaded with a lot of inappropriate material,

but everyone has a different tolerance level, so I always say to err on the side of caution. After all, there are a lot of other things to do in Pleasure Island.

While the club has anywhere from four to five scheduled shows per evening in a 200-seat club, the lines start building up early, so plan ahead. Come at least 15 minutes ahead, and probably more like 30 minutes ahead of time on busier nights if you want to get a seat. Don't worry—the bandstand nearby plays music videos, so you have some entertainment to keep you busy during your wait. And you prepared to stand in lines at Walt Disney World anyway, didn't you?

Mannequins Dance Palace

By far the best dance club in the entire complex, the large rotating floor, the thumping dance music, and the blinding banks of synchronized lights make for a metropolitan, contemporary dance scene. While kids can enter other clubs with their parents, only those 21 or older can enter Mannequins from Thursday through Saturday. This makes it a great place to go if you are looking for an adults-only night out on the town. We rate it the best club in the entire complex, though don't come here if you want to have a conversation!

Missing Link Sausage Company

A stand serving basic burgers, dogs, and Philly cheese steak sandwiches, which are surprisingly good. There are no tables inside, but there are some seats outside. See Chapter 3 for a review of this and other restaurants.

FAVORITES AT DOWNTOWN DISNEY

Here are our favorite spots in Downtown Disney:

Club in Pleasure Island: Mannequins

Even if you have no intention of dancing, you have to come in here. The synchronized light banks, rotating dance floor, and great people watching are the best in all of Downtown Disney

Full Restaurant: The Café at Wolfgang Puck

A great place for families, groups, or a romantic date. The menu is diverse enough, the prices won't make you cry, and you won't feel bad if you didn't put on a coat and tie.

Fast Food: The Earl of Sandwich

Real sandwiches, with piles of meat and fresh breads make this recent addition a cut above traditional fast foods.

Favorite Shopping: The World of Disney

Everything Disney for everyone. If they don't have it, or can't tell you where to get it, it probably doesn't exist.

Honorable Mention: Shopping at the Art of Disney/Wonderful World of Memories

The store has some great books, drawing tools, and other creative purchases, even for the artistically untalented!

Honorable Mention: Gospel Brunch at House of Blues

Powerful singing and great food—enough said!

Motion Dance Club

Current top 40 tunes are focused around an active dance floor in what looks like a converted barn/warehouse that might have served as the home of an impromptu rave in a less Disney-controlled environment. This is definitely a club more geared for teens and early twenty-somethings, with a combination of thumping dance music and some mainstream rap and hip hop.

Raglan Road Irish Pub and Restaurant

Past visitors may remember this as a great place to tune in to some cool jazz, but it is unfortunately closed, pending a retrofit. Look for an Irish themed pub opening in 2006.

Rock 'n' Roll Beach Club

This multiple-floor club has pool tables and TVs everywhere tuned to sports events, and is typical of most sports bars found across the US. The music is a combo of Jimmy Buffet, Beach Boys, and '80s and '90s tunes. Some nights, the bar's bandstand will rock out with a cover band playing much of the same genres of music. The Rock 'n' Roll Beach Club is really just a nice, basic fun bar.

Shopping

Changing Attitudes

This store had some items that we found in few or no other locations, so swing in if you have time. There is some great retro clothing, as well as some funny Disney attire with a bit more attitude than you are accustomed to seeing elsewhere. This is a great stop for teens, especially those looking for some Mickey clothing that is a little more edgy.

DTV Gift Shop

The sports themed attire sold here is the same as is found throughout many other stores around Walt Disney World, so you may want to pass on this shop.

D-Zerts

Pretty much what the name says, desserts and some elaborate coffees.

Orlando Harley-Davidson (Formerly Mouse House)

This is actually worth the visit, for a selection of HD attire and collectibles, and other items of interest.

Reel Finds Gift Shop

A lot of movie-related items, such as little plastic Oscar statues dedicated to different "bests," are sold here. Most visitors agree that nothing really screams out "BUY ME!"

Superstar Studios

It is time for you to find out if you really have what it takes to be a rock star! Cut an audio or video track to your favorite song, either solo or with your whole group. This is fun for teens, as long as you don't stand around and embarrass them.

Marketplace

The Marketplace used to be the only thing that existed in what is now Downtown Disney. In the days when it was simply known as "Lake Buena Vista," this area held little more than a few stores selling amenities, some Disney attire shops, and a few restaurants. Times have changed, and it is now the best place to go if you are looking for a particular Disney item to purchase. The food is even better, with a couple of fast food choices, more full-service restaurants, and some places to get snacks. So shop, relax, and enjoy.

note Keep these Marketplace notes in mind during your visit:

- ATMs are located by Once Upon a Toy and World of Disney
- Shopping is open from 9:30 a.m. to 11:00 p.m.
- Buses are located by the Art of Disney

Entertainment/Dining

Cap'n Jack's Restaurant

Cap'n Jack's is a long-standing part of Downtown Disney, and Lake Buena Vista before that. The lunch and dinner selections are seafood heavy, though there are a few non-seafood selections.

Earl of Sandwich Restaurant

This newer entry to the Marketplace landscape builds some great sandwiches, particularly with roast beef. You are technically in a fast food restaurant with a deli-style menu, but the food here sets the bar for what we should all expect in quick service dining.

Entertainment Theater

Across from the World of Disney is a small performance stage where kid-friendly performances occur on a regular basis. Check the sign out front for times and show descriptions.

Fulton's Crab House

Enjoy crab and other seafood dishes aboard a riverboat. This is a popular destination, so Advanced Reservations are a must.

Ghiradelli Soda Fountain & Chocolate Shop

This is the best sweet stop in all of Downtown Disney. The famous west coast chocolate maker offers great shakes and other desserts in this soda fountain that fills up with families satisfying their sweet cravings.

Marina and Boat Rental

You can rent a variety of boats for fun on the lake. Prices vary, as do minimum rental times, but if you have part of your group griping that a day at the Marketplace is like taking a day at the mall back home, you can show them a fun "ride" without having to spend another $50 to get into the parks.

McDonald's

Come on, it's a McDonald's. You know the menu, and sometimes the fries are just what the doctor ordered.

Portobello Yacht Club

Italian is the order of the day, as you can sample the best of the Mediterranean in a comfortable full-service restaurant setting. The club is a bit expensive, so it can seem like a bad choice after bagging a few hundred dollars of Mickey merchandise, but the food is good. Open for lunch and dinner.

Rainforest Café

This chain restaurant with full-menu table service brings a broad array of selections in a jungle setting. The food is good, and the atmosphere offers a great set of distractions for kids.

Wolfgang Puck Express

This express café is very similar in types of food offered at the Wolfgang Puck Café, but the restaurant is smaller, and with a more limited menu. The Express does, however, offer some unique, packaged snacks that might be good to take with you to the parks.

Shopping

Arribas Brothers Glass Studio

Glass art creations from European artisans have been here for years, so there must be quite a demand for their creations. It is also a place where you can watch artisans at work, and there is also a nearby custom T-shirt stand that makes some airbrushed, personalized T's with your own message.

The Art of Disney Gallery and Shop/Wonderful World of Memories

These stores offer a great deal more than their names might imply. Yes, you can buy some of the more expensive art, cartoon cells, and statuettes that Disney offers in a few other sites throughout Walt Disney World. But these stores are a must-do for the items at the other end of the price spectrum. The gallery and store also have a great array of books, art kits, drawing instructional materials, and scrapbooking supplies that will be of interest to most guests. If you want to find a way to memorialize your vacation, swing by here and pick up a few things to mix in with the photos for your album of the vacation.

Basin Bathroom Products Shop

Basin has a unique array of bathroom products that are all chemical free. Their selection of shampoo and soap bars, bath bombs (bath salt-like balls that fizz as they dissolve scents and oils into your bath), and other items are both aromatic as well as good for your skin.

Disney Pantry

With particular focus on the kitchen and bath, there are some fun items also for some house upgrades, such as drawer handles you can buy for your kid's dresser. The kitchen items are of a good quality, and you should also look at the bath and bedroom items, many of which are appropriate for more than just a kid's bathroom.

Disney's Days of Christmas Gift Shop

It is Christmas 365 days a year, and now you can select that Christmas ornament, nativity scene, or Disney stocking that you have been looking for. There is also a section of Hanukkah items.

Disney Pin Traders

Pin trading is a popular activity that is a high priority for Disney. Pins are often an added "benefit" to a vacation package, and are sold throughout Walt Disney World. Guests are encouraged to trade pins they have with cast members (Disney employees), and Disney has even gone to lengths to have a selection of rare, limited print run pins made to build the excitement. This partially outdoor store tries to capture a flea market feel, complete with vendors hawking their own collections on pedestal tables in an adjacent courtyard. If you are an avid pin trader, this is a great stop.

Disney Tails

Disney for your pet. Dog and cat heaven, complete with food bowls, clothing, chew toys, and some cute elastic Mickey ears that your dog may keep on for about 15 seconds. I always wondered why Goofy (a dog) could talk, and was Mickey's friend, but Pluto (also a dog) was mute, and was Mickey's pet. Confusing.

Goofy's Candy Co.

How long has it been since you have eaten something sweet? 10 minutes? 15? Well, if you are in need of candy or other snacks, swing by this store. It has been recently renovated, and offers even more sweet temptations.

LEGO Imagination Center

This LEGO store, recently renovated, brings the full range of the maker's products, including toys for kids well into their teens. The playground outside where kids can climb on LEGO structures and build their own creations is also a popular place to let the kids go free, and it is free to do! This playground area is a hidden treat for families!

Once Upon a Toy

Okay, the toy selection is mostly focused on Disney items, but you will find a bit more than just that. There are Baby Einstein videos (now a Disney-owned product, apparently), Disney Pez dispensers, and *Star Wars* toys, just to name a few. A special treat for girls and boys are the build-your-own Mr. Potato Head and My Little Pony areas, where you can build either toy, complete with Disney themed attachments such as mouse ears. This is certainly a unique item that I have never seen outside of Walt Disney World, except in their New York City store. Think what a great conversation piece a Mr. Potato Head with Mickey ears would be on your desk at work!

> **tip** It is certainly hard not to give in to the little ones as they beg to buy that Buzz Lightyear shirt that they see in the theme parks. But if you can do so, get them to wait until you get to the Marketplace. This collection of stores has the largest selection of items available in all of Walt Disney World, and they may find something even better than what they may originally have spotted. With the exception of some theme-park or attraction specific materials, you will probably find most everything here. Think about coming here earlier in your vacation so that they can understand why that is a good idea.

Pooh Corner Gift Shop and Toy Store

Everything here is about Pooh, Tigger, or one of his other friends. Ranging from housewares to attire and with something for all ages and price ranges, this store has a nice selection.

Summer Sands Swimwear and Clothing Store

Did you forget your swimsuit? This is the store for you. There are also some nice, non-mice, casual clothing options here for adults.

Team Mickey Athletic Club

Golf, football, baseball, NASCAR, ESPN clothing—you name it, they've got it. This store offers some great clothing options, particularly for adults who did not find that "just-right" item at the World of Disney store.

World of Disney Store

Welcome to the mother of all Disney stores! This store has more Disney-logo'd items for sale than any other store in the world! Clothing, house wares, jewelry, toys, CDs, DVDs, *everything*! If you are in the Marketplace, you probably came to shop, and if you came to shop, this is your first, best, and last stop.

To do list

- ❏ Decide which areas of the BoardWalk you want to visit, and when you want to visit them
- ❏ List the places and activities you want to visit
- ❏ Make Advanced Reservations for meals, as necessary

BoardWalk

The BoardWalk is Disney's homage to the Atlantic seaboard resorts of the late 1930s. Organized in a crescent around a lagoon, and within walking distance of both the Epcot and Disney-MGM parks, this is becoming the heart of Walt Disney World. Okay, the "nightlife" here is not exactly fast paced, but there is fun to be had by all ages, if you just know where to look. If you come to Walt Disney World for more than just a day or two, make sure to schedule at least one evening here.

The stores, clubs, and restaurants of the BoardWalk are listed here in order as you walk from the Atlantic Dance Hall at one end to the ESPN club at the other end.

note Keep these items in mind during your visit to the BoardWalk:

- Fun transportation rentals such as surrey bikes can be rented at the central point of the BoardWalk
- Some clubs charge admission on select evenings, so check ahead for rates
- BoardWalk is fun at night, but pretty quiet until then, so don't plan an afternoon here, as little is going on

Atlantic Dance Hall

Anchoring one end of the BoardWalk, this dance hall is hard to miss, especially with the story-high lettering along the roof. The music ranges across generations, but it is always a fun, romantic setting. With two floors of quiet, cozy nooks and decks overlooking the lagoon, this is a great date place. And later in the evening, when it gets heated up, the Atlantic becomes a fun, loud, dance hall.

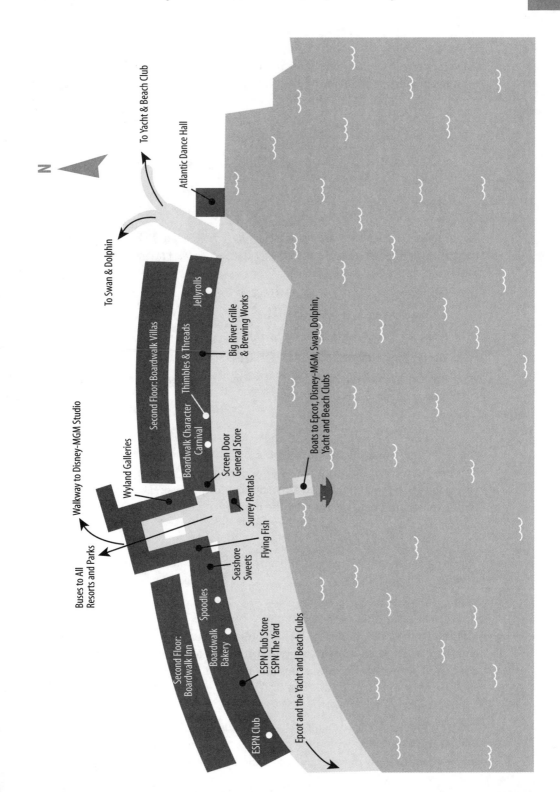

N

To Yacht & Beach Club

Atlantic Dance Hall

To Swan & Dolphin

Walkway to Disney-MGM Studio

Second Floor: Boardwalk Villas

Boardwalk Character Carnival

Thimbles & Threads

Jellyrolls

Big River Grille & Brewing Works

Wyland Galleries

Screen Door General Store

Surrey Rentals

Flying Fish

Buses to All Resorts and Parks

Seashore Sweets

Boats to Epcot, Disney-MGM, Swan, Dolphin, Yacht and Beach Clubs

Second Floor: Boardwalk Inn

Spoodles

Boardwalk Bakery

ESPN Club Store

ESPN The Yard

Epcot and the Yacht and Beach Clubs

ESPN Club

Jellyrolls

Do you like your music from a live person, and not a CD player? Jellyrolls is the most lively joint on the BoardWalk. With piano players going at it, and you singing along, this is a BoardWalk Must-do for anyone looking for a lively, festive time.

TAKE A BREAK ON THE BOARDWALK!

The activity level may be high throughout Walt Disney World, but the BoardWalk is a throwback to a quieter, slower time. That makes it a perfect place to relax a little. What can you do to take a break? Here are some great relaxing distractions

* Rent a surrey bike and ride around the BoardWalk and see the sights
* Join one of the crowds enjoying a street magician, musician, or juggler
* Sit outside and enjoy a beer at the Big River Grille & Brewing Works
* Visit the fortune teller, carnival games, or caricaturist on the BoardWalk
* Grab something sweet from Seashore Sweets or the Boardwalk Bakery and have a seat outside and watch the crowd pass by

Big River Grille & Brewing Works

This microbrewery-restaurant serves up some passably good craft beers, as well as very good selection of light entrees. Wraps, sandwiches, and other foods are better than average and a good value for the money.

Thimbles and Threads Clothing and Swimwear

This is a convenient site for you to get a swimsuit if you left yours at home, as well as a selection of clothes.

BoardWalk Character Carnival

More character attire and toys, there is little of note here that could not be found elsewhere throughout numerous stores, with the exception of some drawings of the BoardWalk that make for nice keepsakes from your vacation.

Screen Door General Store

You can find your basic amenities here, including some pricey foodstuffs. But if you are in one of the suites with a kitchenette in the BoardWalk or Beach Club Villas, this worthwhile convenience could be a lifesaver.

Wyland Galleries

Sculpture and paintings, primarily with a nautical theme, by the renowned artist Wyland populate this gallery.

Surrey Rental

You can rent these multiple seat surrey bikes in the courtyard at the center of the BoardWalk. If you are here with a group of four or more, this is a must. Every fun moment together doesn't have to be on a rollercoaster. You can gently pedal around the lagoon, ringing the bell for pedestrians to get out of the way, and reliving the day's events.

note Don't miss these Must-Do! activities at the BoardWalk:

Jellyrolls

Surrey rides on the BoardWalk

Flying Fish Café

This is one of the best restaurants in all of Walt Disney World, as long as you want seafood. The prices are correspondingly high, but the selection, preparation, and service is worth it. The Flying Fish is a popular site for business dinners and romantic getaways. Open for dinner.

Seashore Sweets

This smaller storefront is decorated with the photographs of all of the Miss America winners, dating back to the '20s. The store has a variety of sweets including freshly scooped ice cream. Skip the sweets from the stands on the BoardWalk and find exactly what you want here.

Spoodles Restaurant

This restaurant features cuisine from around the Mediterranean Sea, particularly focusing on Italian cuisine. This restaurant has gone through many changes, and its offerings can be kind of hit-or-miss. But Spoodles is affordable, and is a popular dinner location, so make Advanced Reservations if you want to eat dinner here. Open for breakfast and dinner.

Boardwalk Bakery

The bakery is a great place for a quick breakfast if you are staying at a hotel in the area. A quick pastry or bagel could be a good choice, but the egg and ham burrito is a cheesy and surprising favorite. At other times throughout the day there are other great treats, sweet and otherwise, and it is fun for kids to watch the goodies being made in the large viewing kitchen.

ESPN Club Store—ESPN The Yard

The store has a variety of ESPN-themed merchandise, which is found only in a few other stores throughout Walt Disney World. The attached arcade, The Yard, offers a limited number of large screen video games, usually of a sports theme. Kids and adults alike will enjoy the Yard, just to see what other sports they have found a way to turn electronic.

ESPN Club

The club has many areas, constantly changing, but the constant theme throughout is that you are never far from a TV featuring one of the ESPN stations. The club offers a basic sports-bar menu of sandwiches and other entrees, but is billed as "entertainment" and not as a restaurant; so while the food is okay, it is a destination for the atmosphere, not the cuisine.

Stands along the BoardWalk

To really build on the atmosphere, the BoardWalk is lined with food and drink stands, carnival attractions, fortune tellers, and caricaturists. This is part of the fun, though you do have to pay to play, so check the prices first. The entertainment is special fun, particularly the jugglers and magicians.

Summary

Nightlife is no longer a dirty word at Walt Disney World! Now you know how to go out and enjoy yourselves, so do it! That just leaves one more set of attractions to consider: EVERYTHING ELSE! Let's move on to the next chapter and consider Disney's water parks, as well as all the other fun that is available. At the same time, let's get an overview of what we might be up for elsewhere in Orlando, and then we will have all the information we need to finish up our planning.

9

Everything Else in the World: Water Parks and Other Theme Parks

Well, after all of the excitement of the four theme parks and the two nightlife districts that Disney has thrown your way, what else could you possibly want to do in Orlando? Well, if you are not yet filled up with fun, there are still a few more options at your fingertips.

After all, what kind of time could you have in Florida if you didn't dip your toes into the ocean and get a little relaxing beach time? It's okay that the beaches of the Atlantic and Gulf of Mexico are hours away. Disney has two water parks that will help you daydream that you are there, complete with snorkeling and surfing.

And what about those of you that are looking for some time away from Mickey Mouse? Well, Orlando is the world's capital of theme parks, and they are not all from Walt. There are traditional theme parks, animal sanctuaries turned into amusement parks, and even a chance to swim with dolphins.

Listed in this chapter are brief descriptions of the Disney water parks, sports attractions, as well as some of the major non-Disney theme parks and attractions. After each venue we rate it for different age groups, just like we did the attraction ratings in the theme park chapters.

These parks and other Orlando-area attractions might serve as great getaways from the Disney routine, or a great bonus day for your vacation. So take a look at just a small taste of what Orlando has to offer!

Things You'll Need

- ☐ Your Travel Planning Trip Cards
- ☐ Pen or pencil

Blizzard Beach

The Blizzard Beach water park combines a cool ski lodge atmosphere with the refreshing escape from the Florida heat by way of slides, pools, and other water-powered fun. Probably the nicest surprise for visitors is the chairlift that takes you to the top of the rides, replacing the long stairway that you usually find at water parks back home.

The *Summit Plummet* is the signature slide here, bringing you to high speeds (more than 50 mph) as you shoot down the ski jump at the top of the hill. Other "thrill" rides here include the *Slush Gusher*, *Downhill Double Dipper*, *Runoff Rapids*, *Snow Stormers*, and the most social of all, the *Toboggan Racers*. In the last one, you can race your friends in one of eight side-by-side lanes.

If you are looking for a ride you can take together with your family, *Teamboat Springs* gets you on a raft with the rest of your group for a long curvy ride down to the bottom of the mountain, with a little thrill along the way.

For quieter times, there is the *Cross Country Creek*, a lazy river for tubing and catching some rays. There is also *Melt-Away Bay*, a beach area with some lighter wave action to make you feel like you are at the shore.

To the left of the entrance is *Tike's Peak*, an area for little children to get to do what the big kids do. Nearby is also the *Ski Patrol Training Camp*, an area for slightly older kids, usually in the 8- to 10-year-old range. These two areas make it the better of the two Disney water parks for families with small children, though Typhoon Lagoon has its kid-oriented fun as well.

Blizzard Beach also shares a parking lot with the *Winter Summerland Miniature Golf*, a Santa Claus-themed miniature golf course.

> **note** Both Blizzard Beach and Typhoon Lagoon offer basic counter service food, including hamburgers, pizza, and all of what you would expect, but not much more.

🚲 =5   🚲 =5   🛹 =5   🏍 =4   🛺 =3

🚲 = Ages 0-6   🚲 = Ages 7-11   🛹 = Ages 12-19   🏍 = Ages 20-49   🛺 = Ages 50+

Typhoon Lagoon

Typhoon Lagoon offers a different set of water fun, with the centerpiece being a gigantic surf pool. This simulated oceanfront is realistic, with a nice beachfront area for relaxing at one end and controlled wave-makers at the other end making waves tall enough to surf on. These are some pretty big waves, so keep an eye on the little ones.

Like Blizzard Beach, Typhoon Lagoon has a number of water slides, including *Humunga Kowabunga*, *Storm Slides*, *Mayday Falls*, *Gangplank Falls*, and *Keelhaul Falls*. There is also a new ride, the *Crush 'n' Gusher*, which is a single-rider raft thriller. The park also has some kid-specific areas, such as *Ketchakiddee Creek*, for little ones up to 6 years old.

Typhoon Lagoon also offers some unique attractions, including the *Shark Reef* salt water snorkeling area, complete with actual sharks, and the lazy winding *Castaway Creek* for a relaxing tube ride around the water park.

tip Perhaps the coolest attraction at Typhoon Lagoon is the surfing lessons. That's right, *surfing*! Before the park opens up to guests, a reservations-required group is brought in and taught how to surf, using the six-foot-high waves of the Surf Pool. Where else will you get such great conditions to learn? For pricing and reservations, call 407-WDW-PLAY (407-939-7529).

🚲 =4   🚲 =4   🛹 =4   🏍 =4   🚜 =3

WHICH WATER PARK SHOULD I CHOOSE?

Blizzard Beach is probably most groups' best bet, since it has two areas for kids of different ages, as well as the better selection of water slides. The fact that it also has a miniature golf park right outside its gates is a plus if someone grows tired of the water fun. Some will find Typhoon Lagoon better for a few reasons, including the snorkeling in the *Shark Reef*, the more realistic waves on the surf pool, or for the surfing lessons. You just have to decide what your group's interests are.

While admission to the water parks is usually included in many of the ticket packages from Disney, if you have to pay separately, it is $34 for a single day pass, $28 for kids aged 3–9.

🚲 = Ages 0-6   🚲 = Ages 7-11   🛹 = Ages 12-19   🏍 = Ages 20-49   🚜 = Ages 50+

Sports, Spas, and Other Fun and Games at Walt Disney World

A day watching spring training or lounging at the spa, a round of golf, or some other recreational activity at Walt Disney World can help make it a perfect vacation for everyone. The following sections talk about some of the best sporting (and non-sporting events) offered at Walt Disney World.

> **note** For more information about activities such as boating, horseback riding, tennis, and others, visit www.waltdisneyworld.com; and make reservations at 407-WDW-PLAY (407-939-7529).

Disney's Wide World of Sports Complex

This Disney sports facility brings together professional-quality sports fields and other facilities to support a variety of sporting events, as well as the All Star Sports Café. The locale is known for hosting a variety of youth sporting tournaments for soccer, softball, and baseball, as well as marathons and other sporting events. Perhaps the best known use of these impressive sports facilities is as the Spring Training home of the Atlanta Braves. Call 407-839-3900 or Ticketmaster for tickets, which range from $13 to $21.

> **note** There is an *Official All Star Café* restaurant and bar in the complex. The problem is that it is either packed because there is an event, or it seems abandoned because *nobody* is there. If you are there and need something to eat, this café is great. But don't make a special trip here, as it can be a bit depressing to be eating alone in a deserted restaurant.

Richard Petty Driving Experience

You can actually drive a NASCAR-style race car at the Walt Disney World Speedway, which is located near the entrance of the Magic Kingdom. There are several experiences available that can either place you behind the wheel or in the passenger seat. You can learn more about these different options, their costs, and their time duration, as well as make reservations at 800-237-3889.

WDW Golf Courses

With 99 holes of golf around Walt Disney World, there are a lot of high quality links for a duffer. For golf tee times, call 407-938-GOLF (407-938-4653).

- Eagle Pines
- Osprey Ridge
- Lake Buena Vista

- Palm
- Magnolia
- Oak Trail (9-hole walking course)

Spas at Walt Disney World

Two resorts offer major spas, while 6 others offer limited spa services.

Here's a list of the full-service spas:

- Grand Floridian Spa and Health Club (call 407-824-2332 for reservations)
- The Spa at Disney's Saratoga Springs (call 407-827-4455 for reservations)

Spa services also are offered at these locations:

- Disney's Animal Kingdom Lodge
- Disney's BoardWalk Inn
- Disney's Contemporary Resort
- Disney's Coronado Springs Resort
- Disney's Wilderness Lodge Resort
- Disney's Yacht Club Resort

Disney Cruise Line

Disney operates two cruise ships, the Wonder and the Magic, which are usually cruising in the Caribbean and along the Florida coastline. These two liners offer many different package options that can either be a cruise-only experience, or can pair some boat-time with a Walt Disney World vacation. These custom-built boats are great for families that want to try out the cruise experience. As much as they try to also make the cruises attractive for adults, they are definitely focused to groups with kids, and may not be the best bang for the buck for adult-only groups. Find out more, and price out options at www.disneycruise.com.

> **tip** Disney even operates its own island retreat, Castaway Cay, which is filled with activities for all ages.

Other Theme Parks

Walt Disney World is only one of the theme parks that call the Orlando area home. This section gives you a quick overview of some of the others.

Universal Studios

This is the lead competitor to Walt Disney World in the Orlando area, and if your group is up for more thrill rides, this might be a good side trip on your vacation. Great rides such as the *Incredible Hulk Coaster* and *The Amazing Adventures of Spider-Man* take both the roller coaster and 3D ride simulators to hair raising levels. If you have older teens who you think might want for some more up-tempo thrills, or especially if you have an all-adult group similarly inclined, you should consider at least a day at Universal. There are areas for younger kids, such as Seuss Landing, which is like falling into a Dr. Seuss book. But the adult-focused thrill rides are the main reason to head here from Disney.

Universal Studios is actually two theme park areas, namely Universal Studios and the Islands of Adventure. Ticket prices are approximately $60 for one park for one day, or $105 for access to both parks, for two days. There is no ticket for a single day with access to both parks, though some Bonus Pass tickets have been available exclusively online that offer access to both parks for five days for $99.95, so always make sure you check before you leave if there are any specials. You can purchase these tickets at the gate, but I would suggest that you visit **www. universalorlando.com** to check for current prices and special discount packages.

> **tip** You can buy "FlexTickets" that cover these parks as well as Sea World, Wet 'n Wild, and Busch Gardens. The tickets are good for two weeks, and cost in the range of $180 to $225 ($150–$190 for kids) and also available via Universal Studios. You can order tickets in advance at www.universalorlando.com or at 407-363-8000.

SeaWorld

This aquatic theme park gives visitors up-close and entertaining access to the wonders of the ocean. Long-popular shows with the famed killer whale Shamu, as well as manatees, dolphins, and other displays of sea life from around the world are entertaining and educational all at once. There are also a few rides, such as the Kraken rollercoaster and the Journey to Atlantis log flume. Ticket prices are approximately $60 for a single day ($48 for kids 3–9), and can be ordered in advance at www.seaworld.com or at 1-800-4ADVENTURE (800-423-8368).

Discovery Cove

This attraction is not a theme park at all. Discovery Cove is a relatively new addition to the Orlando area and offers you a chance to swim with the dolphins. It is one of the Anheuser-Busch properties (like Sea World and Busch Gardens) and is located next to SeaWorld. Reservations are required, as only 1,000 guests are allowed in at a time. Inside, there are a number of interesting attractions. Guest can have a

30-minute session with dolphins, swim among rays in their own lagoon, or snorkel in a coral reef and along a lazy tropical river. There is also an aviary and a resort pool, all set in a lush jungle setting that provides a very rare and relaxing experience. Tickets range in cost from $230 to $260, depending on the time of year. This ticket also provides admission to SeaWorld or Busch Gardens for 7 days. Tickets without the dolphin experience are available, and less expensive. Reservations can be made at www.discoverycove.com or at 1-877-4-DISCOVERY (877-434-7268).

Summary

Well, that about does it, right? Not really! There is so much to do in Orlando that it is important to focus on the fact that you can't possibly do it all. Doing what is fun for your group is your top priority. After that you can just plan to keep your eyes open and see what you want to do when you come back to Orlando on your next visit!

Part IV

Appendixes

References and Resources

This resource list offers phone numbers and web addresses that you'll find useful when planning your Walt Disney World vacation. Though there are thousands of such resources available, I've culled the list down to include only those that I think are the most important and useful.

Phone Numbers

Disney Phone Numbers

Central Reservations Office: 407-WDISNEY (407-939-7639)

Advanced Reservations (Meals): 407-WDW-DINE (407-939-3463)

Baby Sitting Reservations: 407-WDW-DINE (407-939-3463)

Disney Travel Company: 407-939-7806

Activity Reservations: 407-WDW-PLAY (407-939-7529)

Vacation Planning line: 407-939-7675

Fishing Excursions: 407-WDW-BASS (407-939-2277)

Disney Cruise Line: 800-951-3532

Disney Vacation Club: 800-500-3990

Websites

Official Disney Websites

www.disneyworld.com—The main website for Walt Disney World

www.disneycruise.com—Disney Cruise information and reservations

www.disneyweddings.com—Planning site for weddings and anniversaries

www.disneymeetings.com—Group and business meeting planning

www.disneyvacationclub.com—Timeshare information

Unofficial Disney Websites

www.allearsnet.com—Deb's Unofficial Walt Disney World Information Guide

www.wdwinfo.com—"The Internet's Largest Unofficial On-Line Guide to Walt Disney World"

www.intercot.com—Walt Disney World: inside and out

www.jimhillmedia.com—Columns and discussions about Walt Disney World

www.mouseears.net—Sound clips from attractions throughout the Magic Kingdom

www.mouseplanet.com—Reviews and chat boards

www.wdwmagic.com—Reviews and chat boards

www.mickey-mouse.com—Park information

www.disneyworldtrivia.com—Trivia about the park

www.magicalmountain.net—Reviews and forums

www.pscalculator.net—Date calculator that tells you how far in advance you can make advance reservations for meals and shows

www.magicalley.com—Park information and forums

> **note** www.zazzle.com— The Disney ink shop at Zazzle lets you make personalized T-shirts with authorized Disney art—a perfect site if you want to get matching Ts for a group with that special Disney touch!

Travel Agency Websites

www.mouseketrips.com—Disney travel agency specialists

www.ourlaughingplace.com—Travel agents

www.aaa.com—The automotive club can have great discounts

www.aarp.com—The retired persons' organization also has great vacation discounts

Orlando Area and Other Related Websites

www.seaworld.com—Sea World theme park

www.discoverycove.com—Discovery Cove Orlando for Dolphin swimming

www.universalorlando.com—Universal Studios and Islands of Adventures theme parks

www.orlandoconvention.com—Orlando's Orange County Convention Center

www.mearstransportation.com—For shuttle and bus reservations, or call 407-423-5566.

Find the Characters

This appendix is a quick reference to some of the places where you will find your favorite Disney characters. While we list a few places for some, it is important to remember a few things:

- At some of these greeting sites, the characters come out on a schedule. They don't just sit there all day long, so swing by and check for the next showing.

- Meeting the characters is a popular activity, so plan for lines just like at an attraction.

- These are not the only places to meet characters, just some of the better-known ones.

- Don't forget to check out what characters are at the different character meals throughout Walt Disney World by reading up on Chapter 3: "Dining at WDW: The Real Magic of Disney World."

Magic Kingdom

Toy Story: *The Diamond Horseshoe* in Liberty Square

Pirates of the Caribbean: *Pirates of the Caribbean* in Adventureland

The Little Mermaid: *Ariel's Grotto* in Fantasyland

Mickey Mouse and Friends: *Judge's Tent* in Mickey's Toontown Fair

Assorted other Characters: *Toontown Hall of Fame* in Mickey's Toontown Fair

Epcot

Aladdin: *Morocco Pavilion* in the World Showcase

Snow White: *Germany Pavilion* in the World Showcase

Hunchback of Notre Dame: *France Pavilion* in the World Showcase

Nemo: *The Living Seas* in Future World

Mickey and Goofy: *Mission: SPACE* in Future World

There is also a Disney Character Bus (English Double Decker) that tours around, with stops at the Showcase Plaza in the World Showcase and in between the two *Innoventions* buildings in Future World.

Disney-MGM

Monsters Inc.: *Commissary Lane*

Toy Story: *Al's Toy Barn* in Streets of America

JoJo and Goliath: *Mickey Avenue*, across from entrance to *Who Wants to Be a Millionaire—Play It!*

Mickey Mouse: *Mickey Avenue*

Disney Friends: *Sorcerer Mickey Hat*

Power Rangers: *Streets of America*

Animal Kingdom

Various Characters: *Discovery Island*

Mickey, Minnie, and friends: *Character Greetings Trails* in Camp Minnie-Mickey

Other Character sites, with changing visitors, include *Rafiki's Planet Watch*, *Dinoland U.S.A.*, and outside the park entrance.

Index

How can we make this index more useful? Email us at indexes@quepublishing.com

How can we make this index more useful? Email us at indexes@quepublishing.com

E

G

I

M

How can we make this index more useful? Email us at indexes@quepublishing.com

presidents
American Adventure, 127
Hall of Presidents, 102
pretzels
Snackapalooza, 121
Wetzel's Pretzels, 161
pricing. *See* **budgets**
Primeval Whirl, 153
priority seating. *See* **Disney's Advanced Reservations System**
prix-fixe menu, 72, 84
psychics, 174-176
pubs
Big River Grille & Brewing Works, 78, 174
Pleasure Island's Irish Pub, 167
Rose & Crown, 74, 124
pyramids
Central American, 114
Coronado Springs, 52
Mexico Pavilion, 74

Q - R

Quality Suites Maingate East, 62

racing. *See also* **NASCAR**
Indy Speedway, 108
Richard Petty Driving Experience, 180
Team Mickey Athletic Club, 172
Test Track Pavilion and Ride, 119
Radisson Inn Lake Buena Vista, 62
Rafiki's Planet Watch, 149
raft rides. *See* **boat rides**
railroads
Magic Kingdom, 97, 106
Wildlife Express Train, 149
rain, 15
Rainforest Café
Animal Kingdom area, 77
Downtown Disney, 80, 169
Ramada Plaza Hotel & Inn Gateway, 62
rates
comparisons (hotel), 43
holiday season, 43-44
peak season, 43-44
regular season, 43-44

record stores
Virgin Megastore, 163
World of Disney Store, 172
Reel Finds Gift Shop, 167
Reflections of China, 126
rental cars, 19
reservations
Activity Reservations, 187
Central Reservations Office, 187
hotels, 41
on-line date calculator, 188
restaurants, 66
shows, 160
residence hotels. *See* **Home Away from Home hotels**
resorts. *See* **hotels**
resort and spas. *See* **hotels**
resources
phone numbers, 187
websites, 188-189
Restaurantosaurus, 70, 77
restaurants
1900 Park Fare, 83
50's Prime Time Café, 70, 75, 135
ABC Commissary, 76
Akershus, 71-72
All Star Café, 180
Aloha Island, 70, 109
Animal Kingdom area, 77, 151
Arthur's 27, 89
Artist's Point, 49, 85
Artist's Pallette, 89
Backlot Express, 76
Baskervilles Restaurant, 60, 89
Benihana's, 89
Biergarten Restaurant, 71-72
Big River Grille & Brewing Works, 78, 174
Bistro de Paris, 72
Bluezoo, 50, 88
BoardWalk Bakery, 79, 174, 176
Boatwright's Dining Hall, 87
Boma—Flavors of Africa, 82
Bongos Cuban Café, 79, 160
Boulangerie Patisserie, 74
budgeting for, 13
Café Tu Tu Tango, 63
California Grill, 47, 70, 82
Cap'n Jack's, 79, 168
Cape May Café, 82

How can we make this index more useful? Email us at indexes@quepublishing.com

How can we make this index more useful? Email us at indexes@quepublishing.com

How can we make this index more useful? Email us at indexes@quepublishing.com

W

Do Even More
...In No Time

Must See

G et ready to cross off those items on your to-do list! *In No Time* helps you tackle the projects that you don't think you have time to finish. With shopping lists and step-by-step instructions, these books get you working toward accomplishing your goals.

Check out these other *In No Time* books, coming soon!

Start Your Own Home Business In No Time
ISBN: **0-7897-3224-6**
$16.95

Play Winning Poker In No Time
ISBN: **0-7897-3340-4**
$16.95

Repair Your Home In No Time
ISBN: **0-7897-3339-0**
$16.95

Organize Your Home In No Time
ISBN: **0-7897-3371-4**
$16.95

Quick Family Meals In No Time
ISBN: **0-7897-3299-8**
$16.95

Organize Your Family's Schedule In No Time
ISBN: **0-7897-3220-3**
$16.95